YOUR FIRST **100 DAYS** IN

STUDENT MINISTRY

AND THE **40 YEARS** THAT FOLLOW

JEFF BORTON

LIFEWAY PRESS®
NASHVILLE, TENNESSEE

PUBLISHING TEAM

Director, Student Ministry
Ben Trueblood

Manager, Student Ministry Publishing
John Paul Basham

Editorial Team Leader
Karen Daniel

Content Editor
Kyle Wiltshire

Production Editor
Stephanie Cross

Graphic Designer
Amy Lyon

Published by Lifeway Press®
©2021 Jeff Borton

No part of this work may be reproduced or transmitted in any form or by any means, electronic or mechanical, including photocopying and recording, or by any information storage or retrieval system, except as may be expressly permitted in writing by the publisher. Requests for permission should be addressed in writing to Lifeway Press®, One Lifeway Plaza, Nashville, TN 37234.

ISBN 978-1-0877-2748-6
Item 005828717
Dewey Decimal Classification Number: 230
Subject Heading: RELIGION / CHRISTIAN MINISTRY / YOUTH

Printed in the United States of America

Student Ministry Publishing
Lifeway Resources
One Lifeway Plaza
Nashville, Tennessee 37234

We believe that the Bible has God for its author; salvation for its end; and truth, without any mixture of error, for its matter and that all Scripture is totally true and trustworthy. To review Lifeway's doctrinal guideline, please visit www.lifeway.com/doctrinalguideline.

Unless otherwise noted, all Scripture quotations are taken from the Christian Standard Bible®, Copyright © 2017 by Holman Bible Publishers. Used by permission. Christian Standard Bible® and CSB® are federally registered trademarks of Holman Bible Publishers.

CONTENTS

ABOUT THE AUTHOR

JEFF BORTON Jeff has been in student ministry for over 20 years. He has served in both small and large church contexts and desires to see them all thrive. Jeff enjoys teaching, consulting, and seeing student ministry leaders develop. He's passionate about discipleship, missions, and seeing students be transformed by the gospel.

Jeff is also the co-author of the book, *Simple Student Ministry*.

Jeff is married to Jen, and they have three boys. They live outside of Nashville, and love the farm life. Together they enjoy football, hunting, fishing, and diving.

INTRODUCTION

HERE'S HOW IT ALL STARTED FOR ME. Growing up, students at my church were "preached at" and sent on many guilt trips about the way we were living. Apart from a few events, we never really experienced intentional ministry. I attended church weekly, but my faith was non-existent. Still, I was convinced that I was good because I didn't do some of the "big sins."

God used the death of a friend and the examples of many authentic Christians to show me that my faith was misplaced and how desperately I needed Him. I gave my life to Christ as a freshman in college, and God called me into student ministry a few years later.

I believe the best days of student ministry are ahead. It's my prayer that you get a front row seat to what God is doing in the lives of students across the world. I've spent more than 20 years of my life serving students, and Lord willing, I'll be doing this until I'm 90.

I've seen God do things only He can do. Watching students' lives change for His glory never gets old; it's the fruit of our day to day labor. But I don't have all the answers. I've been wrong more times than I care to admit. I've made terrible decisions and been unfair at times. I'm still learning every day what it means to be a better pastor, shepherd, leader, and friend. That being said, I hope you can glean some insight from my experience.

This book has been in my heart for a few years. I have a passion to see the spiritually dead come alive in Christ. I long to see the calloused and comfortable transformed into people who are passionate about and hungry for God. I truly believe student ministry is the best place to see this transformation. I'm excited to share what I've learned and to be an encouragement to you as you live out your calling.

HOW TO USE

This book is broken into two sections. The first four chapters cover your first 100 days in student ministry. The focus is on developing your heart for God; becoming a shepherd and a leader. It's honest talk about your own depravity and developing boundaries and leadership skills that can guide you for years to come.

The 40 years that follow are explored in Chapters 5-11. These chapters walk through practical how-tos of building a sustainable ministry. For too long, student ministry has been playing the short game instead of developing consistent, long range goals of raising up disciples that will make disciples.

I know reading a book can feel like a one sided conversation. However, the tone of this book is conversational, more like, "Let's sit down and talk about life in ministry." I'm excited to go on this journey with you.

Let's get started.

PART
ONE

1 EMBRACE THE CALL

"This is the way."[1]

THE MANDALORIAN

THE COVID-19 PANDEMIC CHANGED ALL OF OUR LIVES FOREVER. First responders, nurses, doctors, and others have stood on the front lines, feeling the daily pain of dealing with this invisible threat. Keith Caldwell is a nurse practitioner in Nashville, Tennessee. He has experienced some crazy moments working in hospitals but nothing prepared him for a global pandemic.

Though Keith and his wife live miles away, during the early days of the pandemic, New York City felt significantly close. Each night his heartache compounded while watching the daily news and seeing scenes of bodies being added to the temporary morgue. As the situation became more dire, the governor of New York issued a request that medical professionals from other states come to help.

After prayer and fasting, it became clear to Keith that God was guiding him to leave his home in Tennessee and serve the people in New York City. The task was daunting. He would work in the Covid units of New York City area hospitals for 12 hours a day, 21 days in a row, with no time off. But as a "substitute" nurse, his presence would allow an already beleaguered staff to rest.

In preparation, God did some specific work in Keith's heart. Not only did God call him, but God also gave him peace that if he were to lose his life, it would happen in the center of God's plan. Keith reminded himself often of

John 15:13: the best way you can love someone is to lay down your life for them. Ultimately, Keith's weeks in New York City were successful. God used him to help patients medically and to pray for and encourage them spiritually.

There's a parallel with this story and your story. Like Keith, your desire to serve has you ready to run into the chaos of the lives of students who desperately need to hear the voice of God. Like other student ministry leaders, you refuse to sit on the sidelines as students destroy their lives living far from God.

Since you picked up this book, there's either a desire in your heart to invest in students or to figure out if this is what God is calling you to do. No matter the reason for reading, you are in good company. In your first 100 days in student ministry, one of the most important matters you must wrestle with is your calling. The rest of this chapter will explain why.

WHY YOUR CALLING MATTERS

Each person has a different calling. My friend Shane specifically remembers walking forward at a camp in sixth grade, knowing God was calling him to ministry. But not everyone has an experience like that—many people don't. Maybe you picked up this book to figure out if student ministry is for you, hoping to gain clarity in your calling. Maybe you aren't even in full-time ministry, and you answer the call by volunteering. Every person's story is different, but the passion to serve is the same.

Before we move forward, let's answer this key question: What is a calling? A calling is the belief that God has moved in your heart to serve in ministry. I admit, that's a broad definition, but the key is that you are certain God has given you the desire to serve others for His glory. I love how Howard Sugden and Warren Wiersbe describe it: "For most, there is simply that inescapable growing conviction that God has his hand upon us."[2]

There are many aspects to being called, but answering the questions of who and where is vital. For example, you might be called to a specific group of people, like students. God may call you to a church, or He may also choose to send you to serve an organization. Whatever your specific calling, it all begins with God moving within you to take a step of faith.

It feels like my initial sense of calling came just yesterday. I was a young believer studying business in college. My plan was to make tons of money and serve the Lord doing it. (Honestly, it sounded like a great plan!) I loved Jesus, but my experience with the church growing up wasn't great. I told the Lord I would do anything but serve in ministry.

Obviously, God other plans and I am in ministry today.

I was afraid God calling me to ministry would mean doing something I didn't like. But He changed my heart, and what I am passionate about intersected with my giftedness. Today, I can't wait to go to work.

Several factors led to my sense of calling. God used being a camp counselor, working with students, and genuinely wanting to see them walk closely with God to show me His plan for my life. Relationships with godly people also affirmed this new direction. Several people, at different times, talked with me about serving in ministry. God's Word came to life as I read, and He affirmed this new sense of calling in me. The most convincing proof was that the desires of my heart lined up with God's passion for people. I don't remember the exact date, but I knew without a doubt that God was calling me to student ministry. It took two years for me to finally surrender to Him. Eventually, I transferred to a different school so I could have a more ministry-focused education and discipleship. Changing schools and being discipled have had a profound impact on my life.

God's calling isn't like a formula that allows you to predict the outcome. Sometimes God uses people to affirm in us what we don't see in ourselves. He uses experiences to open our eyes to see needs and find passions we didn't know we had. Other times we get "voluntold" by a leader that we need to serve and God grows the desire in us.

Andrew Bolton, a student pastor and friend, shared his journey with me saying,

----

"God made it clear I was supposed to be in ministry when I was 16 years old. My dad was so proud, but also made sure I knew that I would never make any money. I ran from God's call, eventually wrecking my life and experiencing an all time low. Some time later, I found myself back in church where a college pastor saw something in me that I didn't see in myself. I've been in student ministry now for eleven years."

Here's my point: you shouldn't compare yourself to anyone else. Don't discount your calling because your path doesn't fit a particular mold. You won't have all the answers, and that's okay. It may take years to figure out and respond to your calling. No matter where you are in ministry, strive to continue learning and be teachable.

Here are a few other thoughts on why your calling is important.

1. **Clarity.** Knowing what God has called you to do is freeing. You don't wonder "what if" you could do something else because you know you are doing what you were made to do. Obedience to the call brings a clear conscience and narrows your focus. If you can envision yourself doing anything else, you should probably do that thing instead.

2. **Power.** God always accomplishes His plan. This means He will give you all that you need to fulfill His plan for your life. The apostle Paul mentioned this specifically in 2 Corinthians 12:9-10. Take a look:

But he said to me, "My grace is sufficient for you, for my power is perfected in weakness." Therefore, I will most gladly boast all the more about my weaknesses, so that Christ's power may reside in me. So I take pleasure in weaknesses, insults, hardships, persecutions, and in difficulties, for the sake of Christ. For when I am weak, then I am strong.

---

3. **Confidence.** You can run with confidence knowing the Lord has called you. You can move forward without fear because He is leading you. Remembering that God has placed a calling on your life can be encouraging on difficult days. Knowing that God has called you gives you confidence when you feel inadequate or like a failure. Truthfully, if you aren't called to ministry, there's very little chance that you will stay in it.

Embracing the call God has given you is far more than just acknowledgment. God's call on your life is more than a title or a place on an organizational chart. Every fiber of who you are matters and how you live this life will affect your ability to do ministry. Because this is true, we must pay special attention to our hearts. As Scripture says, our passions and desires come from our hearts, so we must protect it (Prov. 4:23).

PAUSE

I know that as people in ministry we are supposed to have passion for God and the right intentions at all times. Realistically, we know there are times when our faith is stagnant and our hearts become callous. If we aren't careful, our relationship with God can just become part of the job.

Jesus shared a powerful lesson on the condition of our hearts in Mathew 3. For many years, I thought the parable of the sower was only about people responding to the gospel. Now, I believe this passage is also teaching us how believers respond to the work of Christ in us. The soils represent the condition of the human heart and how we respond to what God is doing in us.

Then he told them many things in parables, saying, "Consider the sower who went out to sow. As he sowed, some seed fell along the path, and the birds came and devoured them. Other seed fell on rocky ground where it didn't have much soil, and it grew up quickly since the soil wasn't deep. But when the sun came up, it was scorched, and since it had no root, it withered away. Other seed fell among thorns, and the thorns came up and choked it. Still other seed fell on good ground and produced fruit: some a hundred, some sixty, and some thirty times what was sown."
MATTHEW 13:3-8

Jesus is the Sower and the seed is the Word of God. The soils represent our hearts, their condition, and our response to Him.

Jesus' first illustration is the hardened heart. Because the ground is packed down so hard due to the trampling of footsteps, it is difficult to farm. The seed never breaks the surface to take root, so the birds come along and eat it. Hard hearts are much like this soil. Although God is at work in us, we aren't listening. Our pride keeps us from having a teachable spirit, and we rely on our skills and talents. Although we may be teaching from the Word each week, it's not having an impact on our lives.

Rocky ground is representative of a shallow heart. This heart is well meaning, probably even passionate, but the Word dissipates quickly when trials come. Put simply, when the believer faces difficult days, God's truth is abandoned. Difficulty doesn't kill our faith, it reveals it. The quickness with which we let our faith crumble is the litmus test for how we actually trust God.

Jesus' third example is thorny ground. Thorns show us a picture of a crowded heart. There's good soil, but too many other things in the dirt destroy the seed. John Calvin explained that our hearts are "a factory of idols," meaning we are quick to prioritize many things over God's role in our lives.[3]

We are at great risk because we serve in the church and allow even Christian or church things to take precedent over God's work in us.

Jesus ended this parable by sharing what sensitive soil looks like. Good ground illustrates the responsive heart. Seed takes root and a plant begins to grow. The key thought here is that not only does a heart submitted to God receive the truth, but it also produces fruit as a result. A heart that is humble, teachable, repentant, and willing to obey will be usable by God. The condition of our hearts will dictate how we are used by the Lord.

Too often, we evaluate our hearts by our intentions and by what we are doing "for the Lord" but we rarely evaluate our hearts by who we are becoming. Scripture challenges us to look at our own hearts and to be certain we aren't calloused, shallow, or too busy to grow in intimacy with Christ.

You've probably noticed that knowing a wealth of theology hasn't been part of the conversation to this point. That was intentional. Theology is necessary, and we should continue to learn it. And as we learn, we should be in awe of God. Solid theology helps us know how to live out what's true. But if what we believe doesn't actually change how we live, then our pursuit of more information is meaningless. Our heads can be full of excellent theology while our hearts are far from God. Gathering information and facts about God does not place us in right relationship with Him.

We must remember that information and transformation are not the same. Theology, though practical and necessary, is information about God. I believe student ministry leaders and students should learn theology continually. However, transformation occurs when there is effective application of what we've learned. If you are learning much about God, but your life is not affected on a daily basis by what you are learning, then you are only retaining facts. You aren't experiencing transformation, you're just really good at gathering information.

Your walk with God will determine every facet of your ministry life. We can talk the latest strategies and ideas, but if your heart is distant or disconnected, you've missed the point. After 20 years in student ministry, I've learned that I have to evaluate some areas of my own heart often. I'll share them with you in hopes that you can avoid some of my mistakes.

I RELY ON MYSELF TOO MUCH

I love being in student ministry, and I like to win. I get frustrated when things don't go my way, and because I've been in ministry for awhile, I have a grasp on what works and what doesn't. When things are going great, I sometimes become less reliant on the power of the Holy Spirit and far more dependent on the practices that have brought success in the past. It's easy to trust in my experiences and skill set. The routine and comfort of what I know creep their way in, believing that if I accomplish X and Y, then Z will follow suit.

I've been guilty of planning strategies and details down to the smallest details for events and just asking God "to bless them." Wow! The pride in my heart can be awful. It's almost like I'm saying, "I've got this figured out God. If you'll just put some of your magic dust on here for kids to get saved and to grow this ministry, we will be all good."

Have you ever been guilty of this? Can you say you are truly prayerfully dependent on God for the outcomes in your ministry? I don't mean that you're lazy and ask God to simply make it happen without you having to lift a finger. But what's the condition of your heart? Do you believe that if God doesn't show up, then it's all in vain? Would you even know if God didn't show up?

Here's a thought that has plagued me: How much ministry have I done that is independent of the work of the Holy Spirit? How many times have I done things that were a success but there was no serious prayer or relying on God to move? Is it possible to pull off an event successfully without the help of the Holy Spirit? It's terrifying to think we could be trying to do this in our own strength and calling it fruitful.

I share these thoughts only because I've learned that they go against who God intended us to be. We were never called to shepherd, minister, and lead independent from Him. My prayer is that if I am transparent about these things, then maybe you can be also, rooting them out of your own ministries and hearts.

I CAN MISPLACE MY AFFECTIONS

Ministry has some pretty intense and busy seasons. Other student ministry friends and I often joke, "Things should slow down a bit after this season." They never do. I'm not complaining—that's just the nature of ministry. With its intensity, ministry demands much from us. Having a full schedule for a while isn't a bad thing, but if we misplace our affection toward our work, it becomes sinful. Maybe this has happened to you.

It doesn't take long for priorities to get out of place. Days and nights are spent praying for people, talking about God, teaching from the Word, and pouring ourselves out for the sake of others. The danger isn't in giving too much, but rather that we aren't experiencing God for ourselves. We become experts at filling other people's spiritual buckets while our own well begins to dry out.

It's times like this when we confuse ministry (our work *for* God) with intimacy (growth in our own relationship *with* God). With His name on our lips, our very work is for the glory of God, so it feels like all we are doing is building intimacy with God. But preparing a sermon isn't always the same as spending time with God. As we prepare, our focus is often on who we are communicating to and not the condition of our own hearts

As strange as it sounds, it's possible to be passionate for ministry and not be passionate for Jesus. If we're not careful, it is possible that we can work in ministry but allow our time alone with God and our prayer life to suffer. We can be very busy "doing" while masquerading as if we are walking closely with God.

I believe this happens in part because we see tangible results from our work. We interact with students and their families, and we see God moving in their lives. Students are getting saved, lives are being changed, and spiritual growth is happening in front of us as a result of "our" work. If we aren't aware of who is really at work, we can start to believe our own hype.

Think about it this way. Working in ministry comes with acceptable behavioral parameters. There are things we can and can't do with our personal lives because of our occupation. And, depending on your particular church background, the "don't do it" list is probably longer than the "for sure do it" list. There are many clear—and often many unspoken—guidelines we live by. Don't smoke. Don't get drunk. Don't live promiscuously, and while you are at it, guard your eyes. These parameters, and others, are necessary for effective ministry. Since we have boundaries for our physical lives, why shouldn't we have markers for our spiritual lives? Shouldn't there be warning signs for the health of our spiritual hearts that drive all of our actions and behaviors?

This is why the soil of our heart matters. If it is not carefully tended, we can get caught up in the belief that our work for God is somehow the same thing as intimacy with God. It was never intended for our work to be the avenue into a close relationship with Him. A spiritually distant heart clearly affects how we live, but it also affects how we lead. It's not possible to lead others to a place we have not been. We can't simply explain the way for them.

I like to shop for groceries. If I'm honest, I usually have to ask a sales associate for help finding an item. I don't mind asking for help because it means I can find what I'm looking for faster. But I've noticed that there are two types of associates. There's the type who, although we are on aisle 14, says something like, "Um, yeah (pulls off headphones), I think that's on aisle two by the Sunny D." There's a faint pointing in the general direction, but that's where the item location assistance ends. Slight frustration ensues, and I quickly realize my time is better spent finding another associate to ask. The other type of employee engages in a completely different way. When asked about a particular item, they stop what they are doing immediately and lead me directly to the item I need. (Clearly, this employee is my favorite type.) They aren't satisfied with simply telling me how to get there, they want to show me and walk with me so I don't miss what I need.

You can't just point, gesture, and talk about how others should walk in relationship with God if you aren't doing it yourself. God has not called us to be distant and disengaged from Him simply because we're too busy working for Him. He has called us to walk arm-in-arm with others, growing together in relationship with God. He has called us to lead others toward Him as we walk with Him ourselves.

If you are simply restating things you have learned in the past and sharing information you know, you aren't really leading with power and authenticity. You are unable to impart what God is currently doing in your life because you haven't been listening to Him. You can draw on things from years ago, but not from today. At best, you are passing off what God did in your past as His movement now. Regretfully, you speak with a passive confidence to others about what needs to happen to grow spiritually, but it isn't taking root in your own life. This isn't a sustainable way to lead or live out your calling.

Leading in student ministry requires us to have strong heart awareness. If our hearts are anything other than receptive and humble before God, we are in a dangerous position. We must be uncomfortable with the idea that we are what we do and reject the notion that success in ministry is a litmus test for our relationship with God. The apostle Paul illustrated what spiritual growth looks like in 2 Corinthians 3:18:

We all, with unveiled faces, are looking as in a mirror at the glory of the Lord and are being transformed into the same image from glory to glory; this is from the Lord who is the Spirit.

These verses show the importance of time in the Word. At my church, we often say, "We get into the Word, until the Word gets into us." Nothing can replace our personal time with God. Walking closely with the Lord, especially in ministry, requires consistency, self-discipline and a "whatever it takes" attitude. We must make sure that we don't let our busyness for God, actually keep us from the presence of God. Dependence on the Holy Spirit, humility, and fostering a hunger for God help keep the right priority in our hearts.

I CAN LOSE SIGHT OF THE BIG PICTURE

My grandfather started taking me out on boats when I was five years old. My fascination with motorized water craft began then and is still one of my favorite activities today. Grandpa was always patient with me as I asked questions. He carefully took time to explain what he was doing and why it was being done. He shared much wisdom with me on those warm summer days. At eight years old, he started to let me steer the boat on open water. As I got older, I could take some of the smaller crafts out by myself. For me, an entire day on the water was never enough time to soak in all the fun. It still isn't.

Navigation was very different in those early days. It was simplistic and rudimentary in comparison to what we have now. Today we use GPS screens mounted in the dashboard of the boat to point the way. Even if those fail, we have the same programs on our phones so we don't get lost or run aground and get featured on a boating fail social media page. But, I learned at a young age how to navigate the waters without the fancy equipment. By picking out landmarks in the distance, I can direct the boat where it needs to go. For example, if we were headed back to the house, Grandpa would say, "See that large clump of trees on the right? Head directly to those. Slow down when you see the buoys." The intent was to focus on what was in the distance so we could get where we intended to go.

Long range vision is good in boating, but much more so in ministry life. In ministry, we aren't navigating around sandbars and reefs; we're avoiding pitfalls and failures that can significantly hurt our ministry. Fame, platform, notoriety—whatever you want to call it—is something we must navigate carefully in order to achieve a successful, long-term ministry.

A mentor of mine said it this way, "Don't look to be discovered, be discipled." That has always stood out to me, particularly when talking about the motivation of my heart. It's not wrong to have a huge platform, and it's certainly not wrong to have influence. Issues arise when attention, fame, and notoriety is what's driving our motivation.

Author and counselor, Al Andrews said, "The human soul was not made for fame."[4] This phrase has proven to be true particularly in the ministry world. Great ministry leaders have ended or squandered their ministries in pursuit of building their own platforms. In effect, they lost sight of what they were called to do. Whenever we desire the applause of others as our motivating factor, we have missed the point. Our calling is never about our recognition, but rather making Christ famous. At a conference I attended a few years ago, activist, author, and speaker, Christine Caine said, "If the light on you is brighter than the light in you, that light will crush you."[5] If you seek fame, find fame, and give your fame greater value than Jesus, then fame will destroy you.

Here's another way to look at this issue. Your talent may get you a leadership position, but your character and integrity will keep you there. Walking humbly with Jesus can't be outpaced by our skill set. I've witnessed first hand some incredibly talented leaders receive amazing roles in the church because of their giftedness, but fumble along the way. Serving God requires far more than talent, or even proficiency, in leadership. We must be careful never to confuse giftedness with godliness. Godliness is the ground where your gifts can take root and grow.

Consider David's example. We learned about his heart for God even before we knew his name: "... The LORD has found a man after his own heart, and the LORD has appointed him as ruler over his people" (1 Sam. 13:14). God identified David for his heart, not his abilities or achievements. David revealed his faithfulness while in the fields as a teenager when no one was watching. He faced the lion, the bear, and other difficulties, and God used those difficulties to prepare David to face the giant when the time came. His devotion to God, even in the unnoticeable and mundane, sustained him when he faced Goliath.

David was after God's heart. We are all "after" something. What are you going after? Are you a person after God's own heart or have you lost sight of that? Are you pursuing Him or something else?

As you begin your time in ministry, be faithful in the small and mundane. Seek to grow spiritually, to be discipled, and then let God give you the platform He wants you to have. Ministry is a marathon, not a sprint. Understand that the decisions and systems you put in place now will affect you for your lifetime in ministry, so choose them well. Embrace the call God has given you. If God truly has given you a calling—and you earnestly seek Him—then you can't fail to serve His people in the capacity He desires for you. Guard your heart, be honest about its condition, and trust the Holy Spirit for His work in you and in your ministry.

» QUESTIONS

1. Write out the call you feel God has placed on your life.

Minister, disciple, and make relationship with students so that they may hear the Gospel and have their own relationship with God.

2. Considering the four conditions of the soil, which would you say best represents your heart today? Why?

Probably a mix of the good soil and the path. I have that desire but I have let other things become a distraction.

3. What weakness of yours needs to be addressed? How has it affected your ministry?

My daily walk with Christ. Haven't been walking strong with Christ so I can't hear what he has for his ministry.

4. Have any distractions caused you to lose sight of what God has called you to do? How can you address them?

Losing my job. I saw it more of a job, not a ministry, not part of my calling.

WHY STUDENT MINISTRY IS IMPORTANT

"The failure to invest in youth reflects a lack of compassion and a colossal failure of common sense."[1]

CORETTA SCOTT KING

JOSH WAS LIKE MOST HIGH SCHOOL SOPHOMORES. He loved sports and talking to girls. He also spent time with his friends, all of whom were familiar with God but didn't have a relationship with Him. A few of his friends started attending student ministry services, so Josh joined them. Every few weeks they would get reprimanded after the service for talking too much and being disruptive during the service. At one point, the student pastor finally said, "I love that you guys are here. But why do you like coming? You don't seem interested at all." In the moment the question seemed awkward, but they saw past his words and to his intent. The pastor reassured them this was the place for them to be, but to leave the crazy behavior at home. The boys kept attending and eventually forged relationships with some of leaders who built meaningful connections with them. These leaders visited the students at the places they worked and called them during the week.

Tragedy struck Josh's life when he lost a friend in a gang related shooting. Not long after, he gave his life to Christ and began to change dramatically. Josh started bringing other friends to church with him. Eventually, the five other guys that he hung out with at church gave their lives to Christ as well.

The student pastor began a guys' discipleship group, and their relationship with God began to grow. Before long, a few of them started to serve in various places within the ministry.

During this time, Josh began to sense a call to student ministry. Since he was already serving, he became an intern at the church after high school. Today, he's a middle school pastor with a passion to see students come to Christ and be discipled.

Josh's story isn't unique. We've all witnessed God's moving in students' lives. Seeing God draw students to Himself is inspiring and builds our own faith. Understanding and being able to articulate to others the importance of Student ministry is a valuable skill to have in your first 100 days.

Historically, God has used students to spark revival during some of the most significant spiritual awakenings in history. They weren't just participants—they were leading the charge.

"STUDENTS" IN SCRIPTURE

Throughout Scripture, we also see how God used students to change history. These stories are probably familiar but the truth that these young people were God's Plan A for carrying out His will emphasizes the importance of student ministry. In the same way that God used young people for His glory then, we long for Him to use students for the same purpose today. Here are a few examples:

» **Mary.** Mary was likely around the same age as some high school students when Jesus was born. She loved God and was a person of integrity (Luke 1:30). God saw her as capable and used her for an incredible task. She was courageous in a culture that punished unwed mothers and remained faithful to the vision God had given her by raising the Prince of Peace in her home.

» **Jesus' disciples.** Many theologians believe some of the disciples were older teens or young adults. What an incredible thought: Jesus entrusted the gospel to students who wouldn't back down but would share the truth all over the world. These weren't the theological giants of the day, they were fisherman and tradesman who didn't make the cut for rabbi school. Yet, God chose them and they were instrumental in establishing the early church.

» **David.** Faithful shepherd boy turned giant slayer then king of Israel. He was clearly not without fault, but God used David to accomplish His purposes in the days of the Old Testament.

This short list shows us what we already know: God uses broken, untrained, and sinful students to change the world. When we love students and see the value that God sees in them, we point them toward a relationship with God. God uses students because He sees in them what they don't yet see in themselves. And He's called us to do the same.

NOT A SILO

Investing your life in student ministry is a worthy calling. Programming that is thoughtful and not bound within a "student ministry only" silo serves the entire church body. Throw away the notion that student ministry is some sort of baby sitting service so that parents won't be distracted in church. That couldn't be further from the truth. Resist the urge to be responsible for students' social calendar; prioritize your time and ministry for lasting impact.

As a student ministry leader, you'll remember the times students reached out to you about the tough stuff in their lives, like when they found out their parents were splitting up. Or maybe they have called you, sobbing with regret or suffering from a broken heart. Maybe they were even having suicidal thoughts and opened up to you. These moments remind us that we are "Jesus with skin on" to the broken people we've been called to serve. We are also reminded of our frailty as we offer desperate prayers for students to run from temptation and into the arms of Jesus. Standing with a family at their student's funeral or officiating the wedding from a student ministry graduate reveals the eternal responsibility we have been given.

When people ask why student ministry matters, these are the moments that come to mind. Building relationships and walking through life together are the essence of student ministry. The discipleship of students is too important to leave to chance. Student ministry prioritizes students' spiritual development and provides opportunities that no other place on the planet can give. Even the best coaches, teachers, and mentors can't provide what a biblically focused student ministry can offer.

Jason Gaston, a next generation pastor who's been in student ministry over 15 years, said this:

"When you survey the pages of global history, you don't have to
look far to see that students have long shaped the landscape
of global change. From serving on the frontlines of a World
War to playing key roles in revivals in Europe and beyond, God

*has continuously raised them up and sent them
out to carry the torch for the world to see."*

Today, students in our cities are more globally connected than ever before and more cause driven than anyone could fathom. Imagine a world where the gospel reaches, grows, and sends those students. That's the world student ministry longs to impact on a day to day basis. With an urgent passion to see lives transformed by the gospel, student ministry doesn't just affect homes, it has the ability to change cities, college campuses, workplaces, nations, and ultimately the world. Mobilizing this generation will not happen by accident or by keeping them busy. Godly leaders who are committed to raising up disciple makers will pass the torch to this generation.

So what does a student ministry that embraces raising up a generation of students for God's glory look like?

SEEKS OUT STUDENTS WHO NEED TO BE SAVED

Adolescence is a wild time for students. While that was few years ago for me, the memories are still pretty vivid. The teen years are an incredibly critical time when students are forming what they believe is true about God and how He influences their lives. The Barna Group suggests that 64 percent of people who make a decision to follow Christ do so before the age of 18.[2] These compelling numbers validate our pursuit of helping students come to know Jesus.

Weekly student ministry services provide a great environment for students to hear the gospel. Church services aren't the only place students hear the gospel, though. Bible clubs, sports team devotions, and on-campus school gatherings all extend the invitation for students to follow Jesus.

In my early years in student ministry, I lived in Miami. Schools were tough to engage, but after much relationship building and serving, doors began to open. Initially, all on-campus events were led by students, but student pastors were finally allowed to attend. One year, at Coral Reef High School, our First Priority club was assigned to the girls locker room. Yep, you read that right: the girls locker room. It was small, had strong body odor smells, and there weren't nearly enough benches for the vision God had given us for the school. But students came and kept coming. That year, we saw a coach from the football team, a teacher, and many students give their lives to Christ inside that cramped and smelly locker room.

Student ministry is incredibly adept at doing whatever is necessary to see students come to Christ. A ministry that focuses on reaching this generation is pursuing what God pursues. Each gathering and each presentation of the gospel is a holy opportunity for lives to be changed. Schools, parks, sports leagues, the beach—student ministry must focus on where students are. Most churches only focus on a "come here" mentality, which means they are happy to share the gospel with you as long as you show up to their service or event. We must be willing to leave the church walls to share Jesus with students, but also offer opportunities for them at church. Creative events combined with student services provide an awesome space for students to hear about and respond to Jesus.

CREATES SPACE FOR INFLUENTIAL RELATIONSHIPS

The one word that best sums up student ministry is *relationships*. Simply put, a student's love language is time together. That's why a guest speaker may visit and communicate very well, but students call you in a time of need. Even when you don't see it in the moment, consistently cultivating a relationship with a student pays massive dividends over time.

Volunteer leaders play a vital role in the formation of students lives. We know there isn't any way for one person to know and care for all of the students who attend our ministries. So, when we equip leaders to engage students, the result is more godly adults that speak life, hope, forgiveness, and guidance into students.

Maria was a leader in student ministry for many years. She lost her own son to an accident when he was a young adult. This tragedy led her to a deeper commitment to discipling teenagers. Because she was in her 50's, many of the guys and girls saw her as a maternal figure. Maria taught them weekly, she and her husband invited them over for dinner and would visit them at their places of employment. She didn't have a degree in education or religion, but had a heart to see students love Jesus. Many of the students who were influenced by Maria stated that she was one of the main reasons they stayed faithful to the church. It wasn't the worship team or the teaching (ouch), but the devoted love of a leader. When a leader like Maria has to step out of their role for any reason, you can see the results of their influence by the gap that is left in students' lives.

Student ministry gives opportunities for students to be influenced and shepherded by caring adults, alongside their parents. Student ministries can build a bridge to the family by reinforcing what parents are teaching at home. While many students come from godly homes, countless others have no significant spiritual influence at home. Many of these leaders are their only example of what an adult who loves Jesus looks like. Student ministry volunteers can serve as surrogate spiritual parents for students whose families are not believers. When we recruit and place godly leaders in students' lives, tremendous growth can happen. Studies show that students who have graduated from high school, but not from their faith, say that significant relationships with adults in the church was part of the reason they stayed.[3]

Many parents didn't experience Scripture and discipleship as part of their upbringing. This highlights the importance of student ministry and the volunteers we place in their lives. We should continually work at building a bridge between parents and students through our events and programming in our student ministries.

OFFERS UNIQUE OPPORTUNITIES FOR GROWTH

Generation Z (students born between 1995 and 2015) has many stereotypes, some of which are true and positively describe many of them. However, other generalizations are negative and tend to downplay this group's desire for anything but themselves. Many of you reading this book are in Generation Z and know some of the statements are untrue. There is more to why this generation seems different. In his book, *Generation Z Unflitered*, Tim Elmore says, "If we are honest, the future snuck up on many of them, like it did millions of parents, teachers, coaches and employers. The truth is we were ambushed."[4]

Virgil Smith was only 13 years old when he was recognized as a national hero. On August 25, 2017, in Houston, Texas, during hurricane Harvey, this unassuming middle schooler grabbed an air mattress from his home and went house to house to rescue neighbors trapped by floodwaters. In total, he saved the lives of 17 people in his neighborhood.[5]

Virgil went above and beyond, doing far more than expected to care for those around him. I'm convinced that student ministry leaders believe in raising up a whole generation of students like Virgil who love their neighbors and do far more than culture says they can. Student ministry is a great place to teach, train, and give students opportunities to live out the faith they claim.

Two other characteristics that personify Generation Z are their entrepreneurial tendencies and redemptive spirit. Being entrepreneurial, they are ready to forgo traditional means of education and try new things for themselves. A 2014 study from consultants Sparks and Honey revealed that "72 percent of high-school students wanted to start a business and nearly one third of those ages sixteen to nineteen had already begun volunteering their time."[6] Their redemptive spirit leads them to be inclusive. They are more accepting of other cultures, beliefs, sexual orientations, and so on. Since their birth, the world has been changing constantly. Because of this, they believe significant change is possible.[7]

These characteristics are a huge blessing for student ministry—we can utilize the uniqueness of this generation to engage others with the gospel. Their inclusive frame work helps remove barriers that have impeded previous generations from engaging others. Help them see how to use their uniquenesses by giving students a voice in brainstorming how to share the gospel with their friends. Engage their entrepreneurial side by gaining their perspective on the weekly teaching and services. Don't just tolerate the differences of Generation Z, celebrate them. Offer opportunities for students to use their worldview and giftedness for the sake of the gospel. We could be intimidated and lament that this generation is different; instead, let's see how God has wired them uniquely for His glory.

STUDENTS SHAPE AND ENGAGE CULTURE

A wise student ministry leader is a student of the culture and the students he or she serves. Even though our message doesn't change, our methods clearly must. In a very short time, current crazes fade and are replaced. Songs that were wildly popular six months ago can't even be remembered today. Our culture moves fast and students move with it. Consider a couple of ways methods have changed:

>> Very few students make (or pick up) phone calls. Not so long ago, phone calls were primary method of communication. Now, people communicate through texting or apps.

>> Although the legal driving age is 16 in a majority of states, many students delay the responsibility and don't immediately get their driver's license. This means students rely on their parents for rides.

>> Social media has been a reality for most of all their lives. They cannot remember a time without it.

Our place is to learn and adapt to what's happening around us. Students are already living in that reality. This isn't to say that all of the changes are good or that there aren't consequences, but students are living in the changes. We have the opportunity to shape their worldview and equip them to engage these changes as Christ followers. Their desire to be different and see change along with being Christ followers is a powerful combination.

Jaylin and Jasmine are great examples of students engaging and shaping culture. They traveled to different countries on mission trips. On one particular trip to Mar Rouge, Haiti, they stayed in a village that had no running water. The women and children would make the walk outside the town a couple of times per day for fresh water.

Most visitors to this mountain top community simply lament the fact water isn't more accessible. These girls refused to believe that Mar Rouge couldn't step into the future and offer fresh water for it's inhabitants. After their return to the United States, they devised a plan and went to work. They created a t-shirt that represented the mission they had adopted, had the shirt produced, and then sold them for profit. All proceeds went to putting in a new well for the people of the village. Engaging on social media drew attention to the cause and others joined in the crusade for water. Jaylin and Jasmine engaged local churches, shared the plight of the people and accepted donations. After a few months, they raised $50,000. Shortly thereafter, construction began on the well.

Students often see needs that adults overlook. Sometimes leaders are jaded by age and disappointment so that when ideas do come, they talk themselves out of them due to past disappointment. Because they see the need, their desire is to create a method to fix it.

Student ministry is uniquely gifted to give students the chance to see opportunities, be challenged by the gospel, and creatively problem solve alongside their peers. Many students want to be part of the change, but don't know how. They see the problems and experience the hurt, but lack the ability to engage. When student ministry trains students to use the gifts God has given them to impact others' lives and partners with them, lives are changed on both sides.

THE CHURCH OF TODAY

I remember like it was yesterday being a student in church and hearing these words: "Teenagers, you are the church of tomorrow. You better get your life right." That was the profoundly desperate plea for me to use my gifts for the glory of God—it fell short, to say the least. I didn't know any better at the time. There was little investment in students at my church, so it made sense that my turn to be the church would be in the future. I had no idea what it even meant to be the church.

In case you've missed it, students aren't the church of tomorrow, they are the church of today. The church doesn't have a wait list or a waiting room. None of the commands of Jesus come with a clause based on your age. Is it any wonder why churches are filled with people who don't understand what it means to be the church if they were never taught? I would argue that just because you are an adult doesn't mean you grasp what God intended for His bride to be. How often churches close their doors for good is an indicator that the people in the pews may confuse being at church with being the church.

Student ministry has the awesome responsibility of teaching students what it means to be the church and how to practically live godly lives. All of the planning, programming, and discipleship should lead students to a greater understanding of how to be the church. Teaching students how to be the church involves answering these questions:

> **What does it mean to live out the "one anothers" of Scripture?**
> **Why is each individual and their gifts important to the church?**
> **Why does the church gather?**
> **What's the purpose of the church?**
> **How does the church serve as the bride of Christ?**

Imagine how the church could look in 20 years as a result of your leadership and investment in students' lives today. This is why we can't live for the short term satisfaction. The students we raise up are shaping the future of the church today. We are training them to be the church directly and indirectly, so consider the type of church you want to see them lead and develop them that way.

STUDENT MINISTRY CHANGES US

Hanging around students changes your life in a variety of ways. I have some gray hair that I lovingly refer to as "Anthony" (In honor of one of my more "interesting" students). In spite of the gray hairs, I've learned so much from students. They've made my life better. Many student ministry friends agree that even though we are the ones leading and teaching, quite often we learn from the students. They help us see the bigger picture. There's a lot of hurt and nonsense in the world and most of it is out of our control, but watching as the light bulb comes on for students inspires hope for the future. Their honesty, passion for God, and seeing them walk away from the old life and step into new life is worth everything.

During my ministry, one particular afternoon embodied the full scope of ministering to students; joy, sorrow and hope were all present. I stood in front of a an auditorium filled to capacity. It was my turn to speak, but I struggled to put my words together. I looked down at the suitcase I was holding and back up at the crowd, hoping that what I had to say would bring some peace and give hope.

This wasn't a Sunday morning service, it was a Friday afternoon in Miami. We were in the middle of a funeral service for one of our students, Christian, who had been killed in a car accident the week before. Christian was a new believer. He'd given his life to Christ about six months before and had been baptized. His parents weren't believers, so discipling him was a priority. He quickly became part of the life in the student ministry.

Earlier that summer, he went on his first mission trip with our student ministry doing tornado relief in Alabama. Christian loved it, and we loved having him there. He was so full of life and questions—the kind of questions new believers ask that are fun to answer.

And just like every trip, sleeping bags, suitcases, and shoes were mysteriously left over when the students went home. Oh, and socks, which are always inexplicably wet. Every trip has some weird amount of socks that no one claims even if they have initials on them. Christian left one of those pieces of luggage and it sat in my office for a couple of weeks.

I'll never forget when we heard the news he and his girlfriend were killed when they hit a telephone pole. I had the suitcase with me because Christian was supposed to pick it up from my office at the Saturday night service. He passed away the night before. Holding his suitcase that day was a vivid reminder of the frailty of life and reinforced the importance of what I have been called to do: share Jesus, disciple, and shepherd—even if the timeline was shorter than I would have liked.

In a nutshell, this story encapsulates life in student ministry. We celebrate when a student follows Christ and is baptized. The joys and pain of watching the student be discipled but struggle with their past only cements our calling to care for and guide them. Even tragedy speaks to ministry, and though it is not always death, there is hurt and disappointment. While some could view this story as depressing, I would challenge you to see hope. Here's how: God used student ministry to impact Christian's life for eternity, and He has used it to change the lives of millions. God uses broken people like us to reach a generation far from Him and will continue to do so.

» QUESTIONS

1. Articulate in your own words why student ministry is important.

It gave me a place of community after the passing of my dad. It brought me to Super Summer, 2011 where I would listen to and accept God's call for me in the ministry. It helped me form a friendship + stay connected with my wife.

2. How specifically have you witnessed God changing the lives of students through student ministry?

My testimony.
Aaliyah - becoming more willing to be in social situations + growing in her knowledge.
Alyssa - again becoming more open socially + joining worship team

3. How is your ministry pursuing students who are far from God?

_____

_____

_____

_____

_____

_____

_____

_____

_____

_____

4. What opportunities do you give for students to reach their friends with the gospel?

_____

_____

_____

_____

_____

_____

_____

_____

_____

_____

3 THE MOST IMPORTANT RELATIONSHIPS

> "Time is currency of relationships. There's no way to invest into a relationship without investing your time."[1]
>
> **DAVE WILLIS**

AS YOU ALREADY KNOW, I LOVE BOATING AND HAVE SINCE I WAS A KID. My grandparents owned a few boats so we would go out on the lake when our family went to their house. The boats were located on the canal behind the house. We would take the canal out to the lake, enjoy the day fishing and skiing, then return before dark.

Upon arriving back at the house, it was common for me to grab a dock line and jump from the boat to the dock to tie off the boat. One afternoon, when I was seven years old things didn't go as planned. I took the line in hand and made the leap as the boat crept slowly toward the dock but I lost my footing. I did not reach the dock and I fell between the boat and the seawall. The boat continued it's drift until it was right over me and pinned me underwater. I was terrified. What was only a couple of seconds felt like an eternity. My eyes were open the whole time, and I watched as the boat began to move away. Suddenly, I felt my grandfather grab me and pull me out of the water.

That afternoon was a picture of how my grandfather influenced my life. He demonstrated love and sacrifice and taught me how to do a lot of cool stuff.

His example of intentionality and giving time has inspired how I love and lead my own family.

Relationships are the essence of who we are and help shape who we become. Growing and developing with the people around us should be a natural way of doing life and ministry. Identifying and nurturing key relationships keep us grounded, in community, and is essential as you navigate your first 100 days in student ministry.

RELATIONSHIP WITH GOD

You're probably thinking right now, "Why would we need a section talking about our relationship with God? I'm in ministry, I'll just skip to the second point." I've felt that way before too. But let's take a minute and digest this: people serving full time in ministry (paid or not) can be at a disadvantage. Because we are in ministry, it's easy to give ourselves permission to not fully listen to sermons or teaching. Maybe we write down a few things, but we often do this so we can use it for our own teaching. Most of the time we spend in prayer is when other people are around. Daily committed time in the Word can be hit or miss depending on the season.

Conversations that focus on our most important relationships start with how we walk with God. If we are ministering to others and our own relationship with God is suffering, we are living a dichotomy; hoping people will do something that we are not currently doing ourselves. If I'm being honest, when I miss time with God because I'm busy or out of my routine, it's noticeable. There are a multitude of excuses: work has been demanding, things are happening at the house, someone was upset, and on and on it goes. I've noticed that when time with God is neglected, my attitude changes, I'm less patient, and I see things about myself that I don't like.

Walking closely with God is not keeping a frenetic pace of spiritual disciplines, although those practices keep us grounded. It's not a list of things to do so that all will be good with God. As discussed previously, it's a heart issue. Be careful that disappointments and hurts don't cause your heart to become calloused. We'll experience heartache in ministry, and if we're not careful, that pain can turn into resentment toward God. Unfortunately, we often set ourselves up to experience that resentment, which can stem from unmet expectations. For example, if I endure suffering or if God doesn't provide in a way that I expected, then I sometimes allow myself to be upset with God. I think things like: "I'm serving You, I've said no to other things to do what you called me to do. Why aren't you doing this my way?" Here's the truth, though: God doesn't owe us anything, and He has given us everything.

A TEACHABLE HEART IS KEY

Pump the brakes when you feel like you know it all or even most of it all. Something is amiss in our spiritual life when the Bible feels more like a textbook and the name of Jesus becomes so routine that it no longer moves us emotionally. A calloused heart lets us think that God owes us something because we've surrendered to Him. A teachable heart recognizes that God is still shaping and pruning us, that these difficult moments are for our good and His glory and that we have so much more to learn.

FOCUSING ON PRAYER IS A MUST

In Daniel Chapter 10, Daniel had a vision of the future that wrecked him so badly, all he could do for three weeks was fast and pray. At the end of that time, he went outside and saw a vision of a man that sapped all of his strength. Then he was touched by a hand. He began shaking and fell to his knees.

"Don't be afraid, Daniel," he said to me, "for from the first day that you purposed to understand and to humble yourself before your God, your prayers were heard. I have come because of your prayers."

DANIEL 10:12

So, Daniel had been praying for three weeks, and God assigned this being to encourage and strengthen him. But God had been listening since the first day of his praying. God hears us when we pray, but we are never assured to get an answer on our timeline. God moved as a result of Daniel's prayers, and He will move on your behalf as well. However, He rarely answers in the exact manner and time as is expected.

Prayer can't be over emphasized. Truthfully, I found it much easier to pray early in my ministry. I didn't know what I was doing. I was worried I would somehow split the church. I was so insecure I assumed I would fail. I didn't want kids to die, and no, I didn't want to get fired. All of this would drive anyone to pray consistently. As my experience and confidence grew, I spent less time praying and more time planning. Looking back, I lament

the passionless prayers I offered because I was d
I strive to never do ministry or live a life apart

Daniel is a clear reminder of the power of pr
plead with God to show up and for the Holy Spir
He can. The only win is for people to see God mc
this happened is because God showed up. Des
effective than our best laid plans.

TIME IN THE WORD CANNOT BE REPLACED

I enjoy spending time with my wife. We like to seek out new experiences, restaurants, and travel destinations. Experiencing these things together is special. Enjoying these firsthand is better than hearing about them from someone else. Even the best descriptions and stories can't give the full scope of a personal encounter.

In the same way, we must be sure we don't replace time in the Word with other books or things that talk about God. Other resources and commentaries are great, but the Word is the key way that God communicates with us. Reading the Bible helps us learn the depths of who God is and how we can be more like Jesus. It's difficult to become like someone we don't really know. Through God's Word, the Holy Spirit convicts us, reveals our sin, and reminds us of God's great mercy toward us. Prioritizing time in Scripture gives the spiritual nourishment to lead others well.

Memorizing rather than simply reading passages of Scripture also has a profound impact. If you have never committed verses to memory, I highly encourage you to start. Knowing the Word gives us strength to stand against temptation and helps conform us to the image of Christ. We are also able to take care of ourselves and minister to others when verses are fresh on our minds.

YOUR FAMILY

Before I got married, work consumed most of my time. It wasn't uncommon for me to be out doing ministry five nights a week, often over 70 hours a week. I was having a blast!

I met my wife, Jen, after doing ministry for three years. During our dating season, my schedule came up quite often. I wasn't available many nights because I had work to do. I often showed up late because I tried to squeeze in more work before we spent time together. My thought was, "I'll slow down my work when we get married. Should be pretty easy to do." I don't think I've ever been more wrong.

...married man working in a ...y in Miami, it was very difficult ... off work." Work consumed me, ...loved it, but my immaturity began ...show when I wasn't able to prioritize my wife over my work.

▶ PRO TIP

Just because you get married doesn't mean you will automatically practice necessary disciplines to balance work and family. Those practices must be developed before the big day.

That didn't last too long. Thankfully, I always know how my wife feels about something. I know because she tells me! When she brought up my work schedule, I started listening. Being gone so often from the home and working while I was home was hurting my marriage. I needed to change.

Slowly my habits began to shift, which was necessary and important because I love my wife and family. I realized how many opportunities I was missing with them that I couldn't get back. I had to choose my priorities. Choosing my family was easy the part, but putting this priority into practice was more difficult. To this day, I still have to be wise with how I spend my time. I've heard the following statement many times and it has taken root in my life: "You can lose your ministry and keep your family, but if you lose your family, you have lost everything." What are you willing to trade for your family?

This might sound strange, but I'm not sure there is a work-life balance in student ministry. Many speakers and books say to "find the balance" but that feels ambiguous and simplistic at times. Truthfully, serving in student ministry feels more like managing the tension of work and life. I don't know anyone who "balances" life and ministry because our calling to both our families and ministry is vitally important. It requires keen discernment from the Holy Spirit to know when each tremendous responsibility needs to take front and center in our lives.

That said, God has called you to serve in ministry, but not at the cost of your family. Don't sacrifice relationships with your kids because you are raising kids who belong to someone else. The calling to ministry doesn't include a free pass to neglect your family and leave them on the sideline. Of course they can't be involved in every aspect of your work, but never allow them to believe that others will always get your best and they will only get what remains.

Over the years, I've spoken to many pastor's kids who resent ministry and the church for "stealing away" their dad. Think about it. Almost every holiday is an important time at the church. Spring breaks and summer time, when students are out of school, are the heavy travel times for student ministry. Christmas and Easter weeks are consuming, especially in churches with multiple services. Without great intentionality, the church will get the best times of life instead of the family.

Readers of this book represent different churches and vastly different work environments. Many churches say family time is a priority but fail to make it a reality. Many insecure church leaders who don't have their lives under control assume having quality family time means you probably aren't working hard enough. What a strange and wildly untrue cycle to live in.

You may be at a church that values the staff's time with their families. Praise God! Lead transparently and love your family well. You may also be at a church that values your contribution to the cause more than they value how you lead your family. Well meaning churches say family is important, but their high expectations don't always allow you to lead your family well. Regardless of where you serve, you can lead your family with excellence. Here are some ways to do just that.

>> **Be present when you are home.** If you're on your phone constantly after you walk in the door from work, you aren't really at home. Sure, your car is in the driveway and your body is in the house, but your mind and affections are elsewhere. Don't let your kids grow up seeing their parent always attached to a phone (talking, texting, or messaging). If your boss will allow it, turn off or mute your phone for two hours after you get home each day. These undisturbed moments will allow you to focus on your spouse and kids. Also, it will help you detach from work so you aren't completely consumed by it at all times.

>> **Intentional time with your family will bring far greater returns than just hanging out.** Have a plan to share God's Word—to disciple and encourage them. Even in the busy seasons, you can accomplish much and still have quality time together. Refuse to raise and disciple someone else's kids while neglecting your own.

>> **Use the vacation days you are given each year.** I'm not proud of this, but for many years I had unused vacation days at the end of the year. I didn't get paid for them, and they didn't roll over. Selfishly, I thought it was a badge of honor: I could tangibly show that I was so committed to my work that I'd give up days off. Man, that was dumb. I lost real opportunities to make memories by choosing instead to do what I do every other day of the year: work.

» **Calendar.** Sit down and go over your work calendar with your spouse often, talking through all of your commitments for the next six months. Focus mostly on things outside of your daily schedule like evenings out, trips, nights away, and so on. A six-month review can help you identify the busiest of seasons, allowing your family to plan for that. It helps to balance the tension of calling and ministry. When we look out six months we can plan family time around the busy seasons. For example, one summer our family had a stretch of five weeks consumed by ministry needs. A few camps and other work travel commitments made the whole month completely booked. Because we were looking so far ahead, we planned a family trip before everything got busy. Our ministry was very hectic, but the family wasn't neglected because we were proactive. The tension is much easier to manage when you communicate well.

 **CONFESSION**

I didn't keep a tight calendar for a long time, and many times ended up surprising my wife with nights away for work and trips. Great communication eliminates surprises and allows us to be more intentional.

» **Protect your family.** We usually think of protection in the sense of physical harm, but in this context, we are talking about church life. Be selective with what you share with your spouse and kids. Obviously, you should share more with your spouse but use discernment. Sharing too much can change their view of the church or your pastor. They will slowly begin to carry the weight you carry and won't see the church as their place of worship. Don't misunderstand: I'm not advocating for you to hide anything, rather, I'm simply cautioning you not to distort your family's view of church.

I learned this the hard way. Because of my responsibilities at work, I can often be critical of how something is done. I want to see excellence. I don't like predictability, and I abhor the idea of cheesy ministry. From time to time, I would make comments about what I saw happening at an event or a promotion, and one of my sons picked up on it. There were never comments about people specifically, but how things were being done. That son started to say things like "Hey dad, this doesn't look right" or "Why did we do it that way?"

I was heartbroken. I never wanted my son to analyze church, I just want him to enjoy it. He simply overheard some of my comments and assumed that was how it worked. I am working hard to reverse this thought process with him. I can readily admit it would have been easier to use discretion than to have to do "clean up" later. When you protect your family, you allow them to enjoy church and see it as the place of worship as God intended.

YOUR PASTOR

I've spoken to hundreds of student pastors, and the topic of relationship with the senior pastor is a popular one. If you were to ask 100 student ministry leaders about their relationship with their pastor, you would get as many different scenarios. Many student pastors enjoy time with their pastor: he is a shepherd, and they enjoy serving together. They have a genuine interest in each other's lives, personal growth, and families. I sincerely hope that's the situation that you are in today.

At the same time, many don't feel that way about the person leading their church. Some would say their pastor is distant, not engaged, and almost disconnected from the student pastor. I've lamented while hearing stories from youth pastors who desperately want to have a relationship with their pastor, but he's not interested. For some, well-meaning attempts to cultivate relationship only end in disappointment.

Others would say they communicate often with their pastor, but it's mostly a list of to do's and expectations. It feels like it's just a boss telling an employee what to do. No personal stories or talk about family life is exchanged, and if it is, it's usually one sided with no questions being asked of the student pastor.

Still others deal with a pastor who is manipulative, an emotional bully, and difficult to relate to. There is no relationship between the two, and the student pastor feels lost. In this scenario, the job feels like a chore, and the student pastor is almost always looking for a way out.

Whatever context you find yourself in, there is a way to honor your pastor and to "lead up." We must remind ourselves that we are under that pastor's leadership and umbrella of authority. In Scripture we see a time when David responded inappropriately to Saul's leadership. Saul was trying to kill David, which is a pretty good indication that the relationship "just wasn't there."

So, when David found Saul vulnerable while going to the bathroom, David cut a corner of Saul's robe off. He didn't touch Saul or even confront him— he only cut off a piece of his clothing. But Saul was still king, and David knew better. He felt profound anguish over his actions.

Afterward, David's conscience bothered him because he had
cut off the corner of Saul's robe. He said to his men, "As the
LORD is my witness, I would never do such a thing to my lord,
the LORD's anointed. I will never lift my hand against him, since
he is the LORD's anointed." With these words David persuaded
his men, and he did not let them rise up against Saul. Then
Saul left the cave and went on his way.

1 SAMUEL 24:5-7

David was broken over the disrespect he showed to his king even though Saul had no idea. David knew this action was in direct opposition to the Lord's plan. Though he had serious issues with Saul, David refused to dishonor the Lord again with his behavior.

Regardless of the status of your relationship with your pastor, it's imperative that you honor him. Even if he does things you don't like, it never gives you the freedom to behave inappropriately by gossiping or undermining his authority.

I'm in several student ministry groups on social media and love the conversations about ministry we have there. One afternoon I saw a post from a relatively new student pastor. In summary, here was the post:

 PAUSE

Honoring your pastor and being under his authority doesn't mean you overlook sin. There is no excuse for turning a blind eye to your supervisor for fear of being disloyal. If you know of sin and cover it up, you are not being a good employee or honoring the Lord—you are complicit.

"I walked by one of pastor's offices, and he was
looking at porn on his computer and doing stuff. He doesn't
know that I saw. What should I do?"

I was taken aback by the situation. This young leader had no clue how to respond, and I grieved that the idea of confronting this sin wasn't a priority. But the biggest surprise was many of the responses to this post. Many of the replies said, "It's no big deal, let it go." Others said, "It's none of your business, leave it alone."

Confront sin, especially if it's those in church leadership. Sure, you may lose your job, but you may save many others from destruction in the process.

Stand for what is right, all the time. Jon Acuff, writer and speaker, said this in a twitter post, "Leaders who can't be questioned do questionable things."[2] Moral failures and integrity issues must be confronted. If you find that you are in a position where you cannot and will not honor your pastor for any reason, then it's time to move on. If your passion and vision do not align with his, it's best to take your talents elsewhere. Do not cause division in the church over your preferred style of ministry.

Here are a few ways to honor the leadership that God has placed over you:

1. **Be publicly loyal and privately honest.** This means if you disagree with your pastor, you disagree in private. Be honest about how you feel and why. Don't stay quiet and then complain later because you didn't get your way. When in public, agree with your pastor. If you disagree with your pastor and share publicly why you think he is doing things wrong, you undermine authority. We must be certain that our actions teach others how to treat leadership and how to handle disagreements in a godly way. Being loyal also means you're honest with him. That's the key to loyalty. This means you tell him your issues and concerns without telling others. If you tell others and then your pastor, its not loyalty, it's gossip.

2. **Use the two-minute rule.** If your boss asks you to do something and it can be done in two minutes or less, do it immediately. Not only does this show that you are listening, but it also shows that what is being asked is important to you.

3. **Have a get it done mindset.** You are being paid to do a job, so do it to the best of your ability. Don't rely on the pastor to do your job for you. This doesn't mean you shouldn't ask questions, but the responsibility of figuring things out is yours. For example, when you have an issue that needs to be figured out, don't just take it to your boss, present it, and ask for an answer. Instead, create two or three well thought out solutions to the problem and share them, asking for his advice on which solution is best. This way, he only has to evaluate potential outcomes and can share those with you or steer you in a different direction. Do the things you have committed to do. Don't expect them to give you all the answers or follow up with you several times. Take initiative, plan well, then execute.

4. **Lead up.** Leading up means you add value to the people who oversee you by influencing them. Not only do you support your leader in this way, but you also become an asset rather than a liability. Here are a few ways to lead up:

   » **Lighten your leader's load.** If your pastor is winning, there's a good chance you are as well. It's also rare for you to be winning if your pastor isn't winning at the same time. Find ways to help your boss succeed.

   » **Be willing to do what others aren't.** Your willingness to step up will help him succeed and will set you apart.

   » **Be prepared every time you meet with your boss.** Show up ready to share what needs to be discussed and ready to listen to what he has to say. Showing up unprepared communicates that his time—and yours—isn't important.

   » **Learn his preferred method of communication.** I've had a boss that preferred face-to-face meetings and another who preferred text messages. Another leader wanted bullet point only ministry update emails once a week. Yet another had no regard for email. When I learned how they like to be communicated with, my messages were received. I didn't expect them to like my preference of communication—I adapted to theirs to be effective. Learn how your boss likes information. Is it detailed or bullet point? Do they like chit chat or just want the facts? When do they like to be communicated to? How often should you communicate? If you haven't been able to discern the answers, ask them plainly. Most leaders have a preference and they want you to know it.

5. **Ask how they think ministry is going.** What would they like to see in the student ministry? What do they think of what is happening? Do they like the results? What results are important to them? Are there timelines in their minds? Value their opinions and input.

6. **Keep your pastor in the loop.** Do your best not to surprise your pastor, especially with issues. If there's an issue with the ministry, let your pastor know so he can counsel you through it. It also gives him the opportunity to be "in the know" in case any one comes to him for answers. It's embarrassing to be asked about an issue that you haven't even heard about.

   I was at my first church for about two years when I brought in a band for an event. I had heard some of their music, so I thought it would be a great opportunity for our students. I probably should have known when they put the eyes glowing, smoking skulls on stage that this was going to go badly. Halfway through the first song at the event, I looked at my pastor, and he gave me "you got to kill this thing" hand motion. That band got to play one whole song of their set. I was embarrassed. I should have researched more and asked better questions. More so, I felt like I embarrassed my pastor. Not surprisingly, that never happened again.

Remember, God has called you to that place to fulfill the vision God has given your pastor. The student ministry is an extension of the senior pastor. Most pastors know what they want to see. If they don't communicate it well, then ask. Develop and nurture the relationship with your pastor to the best of your ability. Don't ever sit and wait for him to take the initiative; if you don't sense any movement, you take the first steps.

PARENTS

Parents are an incredible part of student ministry. No doubt there are varying opinions when it comes to parents and their engagement in student ministry, but we should always push to engage them. If you win the parents, you will win the students. Most would agree that just getting students to show up to services or events can be frustrating because the parents are a necessary factor in that equation. Instead of seeing parents as an obstacle, consider how you can win them to be your biggest cheerleaders.

1. **Build credibility with parents.** Being a credible leader in the eyes of parents requires effort and intentionality. What impresses you might not impress parents, so consider how they think and what they find valuable. If you aren't a parent, ask parents you do know about what is important.

   » **Communicate clearly and often, but not too often.** A few emails a week to parents will start to feel like junk mail quickly, especially if the information provided isn't important or pertinent. A good way to tell if your emails are even being read is to use a good mail service that offers analytics. It's humbling when you think you have created a masterpiece of an email to see that only three parents opened it and one clicked the link. Don't blame the parents, you must write better emails.

» **Don't surprise parents.** If you are speaking on a sensitive topic, give parents a heads up so they can make a decision about their student attending. Don't wait until the last minute to inform them of upcoming opportunities. They want their student involved, so make it as easy as possible for them.

» **Call parents when their student gets in trouble.** Let them hear from you what happened and why you made the decisions you did. These calls are intimidating and not fun, but the relational capital will be worth the effort.

» **Create a safe environment for their children.** Parents want to know their student is safe when dropping them off somewhere. While some parents seemingly push their kids out of a rolling car, excited just to have a moment to themselves, every parent wants their kids to be in an environment that's healthy and safe. If parents know you have thought through potential risks and accounted for them, you gain their trust.

» **Present yourself as trustworthy in the small details.** When you are talking with adults, talk like an adult. Dress in a way that shows you are capable of making good decisions. Bathing and proper hygiene are wildly important when proving to parents you are capable of leading. Some would argue, "That's not fair, I shouldn't be judged by how I dress." I agree, but unfortunately, parent's don't follow those rules and the calling you have is far greater than the clothes you like to wear.

To be blunt, I have a hard time trusting the safety of my boys to someone who doesn't brush their teeth or wear a seat belt. If that person can't handle common sense stuff, they probably haven't thought through the responsibility of caring for my kids. It takes years to build honest report with parents, but that trust can be lost in a moment. Be sure to include the influence of parents in your decision making process.

2. **Recruit parents to serve with you.** When parents serve on your team, good things can happen. Parents tend to follow the advice and caution of other parents, so when you are engaging them well, parents become your biggest advocates. When possible, recruit married couples to serve. This gives the family an option to serve together and shows students what a godly relationship looks like. Many students never see how a husband and wife interact in a

Christ honoring manner, so this provides a teaching moment that is "caught" rather than "taught."

3. **Minister to parents.** There are three aspects of ministering to parents: informing, educating, and caring. Student ministry can be guilty of heavily informing parents and not educating or caring for them well. When you are able to do all three aspects, you provide spiritual health for the whole family.

» **Informing.** Informing parents is the easiest and most common way we engage parents. We send an email or text about camp sign-ups or the next big thing, making sure they know payment dates and when to show up. Master the art of communication in this area. Don't just flood parents with info, make it relevant and timely.

» **Educating.** Educating parents can be intimidating, particularly when you are a young leader. How do we teach parents to be a parent when I'm not a parent? You don't have to be an expert on everything, but use people who are.

For example, our student ministry did a training on social media for parents. It was one of our highest attended trainings, which makes sense, because parents want to know about social media. Our team didn't feel equipped to handle this discussion, so we asked a man in our church who works in the area of cyber crime and Homeland Security to lead it for us. It was a home run! Parents walked away feeling equipped to lead their student better.

The keys to a good parent meeting are a time they can engage, content that helps them grow as a parent, and being sure you don't waste their time. A great way to exclude dads from your ministry is to waste their time. But educating can also be done in your weekly update or email. Give book or podcast recommendations that will help them grow. Share a blog or website that has good resources and cost nothing.

» **Caring.** Caring for parents shows that you don't just care for their student, you care for the whole family. When ministry opportunities arise with a family, show up. When you are invited to a family's house to eat or hang out, go and encourage them. When tragedy strikes, be present and bring others to help with whatever can be done for the family.

4. **Respond well to parents.** Respond to parents as quickly as you are able. Texting, calling, or meeting within 24 hours is a good rule.

Sometimes that is difficult, especially if you fear a tough conversation, but showing respect in this manner will go a long way with parents. Sometimes parents get angry. Now and then they get angry and say mean, hurtful things. Be careful how you respond. Commit this verse to memory:

A gentle answer turns away anger,
but a harsh word stirs up wrath.
PROVERBS 15:1

There may be a time when a parent or someone else is loud, yelling, and hostile. This doesn't happen often, but be prepared if it does. Never yell at a parent. Take a breath, step away, and do whatever it takes to keep your composure. If in public, invite the parent to talk privately another time. Don't try to save face while defending yourself—that won't help and you will regret it later. If they refuse to stop engaging, calmly let them know you are looking forward to talking when emotions aren't so high. Potentially, you can lose two ways in this situation. You can lose by responding angrily or by losing the respect of those you serve. It just isn't worth it.

If you have made mistakes, own up to them and apologize. Explain how things will be different going forward. If it's a misunderstanding, without attacking, carefully explain the situation. Remember, restoration will be very difficult if you lash out at a parent. We don't always know what's happening in a home and their behavior may be a result of another catastrophe. Shepherding parents when they are angry takes wisdom, patience, and grace that only the Holy Spirit can provide. Recite Proverbs 15:1 repeatedly to remind yourself of this truth. Remember this common saying too, "people may not remember what you said, but will always remember how you made them feel."

VOLUNTEERS

Volunteers are the life blood of ministry. Ministry is far more effective and meaningful when done with volunteers. Later in the book, we will talk about developing volunteers, so this portion serves to highlight the importance of relationships with them. Here are some ways to cultivate relationships with the volunteers in your student ministry:

» **Think like a volunteer.** I often challenge myself to stop and put myself in their shoes. It's humbling when I pause long enough to consider what people sacrifice to serve. A good leader doesn't take volunteers for granted. I've been guilty of this and have done it more than I'd like to admit. When we view those who serve in our ministry like a piece of an organizational puzzle, we overlook them. Remind yourself that they don't serve you; they serve students alongside you so that students can know God better.

» **Train your leaders well.** The temptation would be to only teach them things that help them be good at church work. We must teach better techniques for leading in student ministry, but should also teach things they can use in everyday life. We don't want to just produce great student ministry volunteers, let's help them thrive in every area of their lives.

» **Engage in the life of your volunteers.** Get to know them as people and what they are passionate about. Meet with them often. Know what's going on in their families. If you serve in a large ministry, assign coaches who will care for the many volunteers since you can't keep up with everyone. Volunteers should know we care more about who they are than what they do for the ministry. A good leader invests in people and has relational capital from volunteers they lead well.

» **Love your volunteers well.** I remember a night I got a call from a volunteer who was crying. I'd never seen this woman get emotional, so I knew something was wrong. She began to share a tragedy that happened at her house. She was letting a man she knew stay in the garage for a few weeks while he was getting his life together. She was older and this was an incredibly kind gesture. However, the man took his life that night and she didn't know where to turn. She asked if we could come over.

Jorge, one of my closest friends and also a pastor at the church, went with me to her house. We listened, prayed, and then we asked if we could do anything for her family. "There is one thing," she said. She asked if we could clean the garage from the incident. She couldn't bring herself to do the work; it was too overwhelming. We replied with: "Absolutely, we will." And we got to work. Never in my life did I think ministry would involve what we were doing, but that night it did.

Caring for volunteers and nurturing relationship requires far more than just saying hello when they show up to serve. The way you display kindness and love toward your volunteers is the example students will see for how to treat them. Love your volunteers well. Be present with them in the dark valleys. When you care for someone, you rescue them when necessary. You move things out of the way so they can thrive and, in return, you thrive as well. Nurture these relationships and protect them. Incredible ministry has never been done alone. As a leader, love and lead those around you into a movement for the glory of God.

» QUESTIONS

1. Which relationships in your life and ministry are thriving and which ones need attention?

....

....

....

....

....

2. How are you doing with balancing the tension of work and family time? What practice works well for you?

....

....

....

....

....

3. How well do you "lead up" to your pastor? How might that relationship need to improve?

....

....

....

....

....

4. What percentage of your work week is spent developing relationships? How might that number need to change?

....

....

....

....

....

4 DEVELOPING YOURSELF

"One can choose to go back toward safety or forward toward growth. Growth must be chosen again and again; fear must be overcome again and again."[1]

ABRAHAM MASLOW

FREE DIVING IS INCREDIBLY FUN. Different than snorkeling or scuba diving, free diving is the discipline of using a single breath of air to explore beneath the surface of the water. The challenge is to learn to hold your breath and explore under water without the aid of any breathing apparatus.

I learned to free dive when I was a kid. There was no formal training—I just tried to get better each summer. During my middle school years, I thought "hyperventilating" would help me hold my breath longer. I'd breathe in and out—fast and furiously—followed by slow, deep breaths for the same amount of time. It worked to some extent, but there was a limit to what I could do. I was hoping to "oxygenate" my blood in the process. In my 7th grade boy mind, it was my path to becoming the next Jacques Cousteau. (If you've never heard of him, Google him. He's a legend!)

While living in Miami and spending considerable time in the ocean, I started learning from guys who had been free diving for years. They taught me about apnea. This is not sleep apnea—which happens when breathing unintentionally stops while sleeping. In the world of diving, apnea is a discipline of learning to slow your heart rate and expand your lung capacity so that you can hold your breath longer and achieve greater depths. Holding my breath longer and swimming deeper meant catching more lobsters and spearing bigger fish.

I didn't master free diving all in one day. It took trial and error—like my attempts to hyperventilate—and learning new techniques like apnea. It took time to develop my lungs and train my mind to think differently. Training started in a pool and then moved to the ocean, as I learned to dive at incrementally greater depths. Over time, I improved but it took years to develop a routine that was consistent and safe. The discipline of learning to free dive helped me train my mind when attempting to do things I thought were too difficult. Each level of training prepared me for the challenge ahead.

Self development is required in many areas of life. Learning new technology, navigating around a new city, playing a video game, and even learning a new sport demands practice and discipline to excel. Having to master new things is part of the human experience.

That same commitment to learning is necessary as you lead in student ministry. You didn't get all the answers when the job started; in fact, that's the first step in the shallow end of the pool. Consistency, focus, and dependence on the Holy Spirit will help lead you to greater depths of leadership. In this chapter, we will look at two aspects of personal leadership in student ministry: the importance of being a shepherd and developing your leadership skills as you shepherd others.

For most, being a shepherd is the primary focus early in ministry. It's what we sign up to do. However, as ministry grows and demands intensify and we face the daunting task of tackling the day to day operations of ministry, shepherding is often neglected. Like free diving, shepherding is a skill that must continually be developed in your first 100 days and beyond.

YOUR ROLE AS A SHEPHERD

We can't talk about being a shepherd without looking to Jesus as the ultimate example. As leaders in the church, our role is to model what Christ has laid out for us. This brings meaning and clarity to our role, especially when we experience points of frustration. Jesus said,

"I am the good shepherd. The good shepherd lays down his life for the sheep. The hired hand, since he is not the shepherd and doesn't own the sheep, leaves them and runs away when he sees a wolf coming. The wolf then snatches and scatters them."
JOHN 10:11-12

In these verses, the role of a shepherd is clear. He provides for and protects his sheep. He leads to them to water, food, and a place to rest. He will do whatever it takes to protect them. These verses also indicate that someone who isn't a shepherd will behave differently. In fact, when danger or difficulty comes, the false shepherd will abandon the sheep in an attempt to save himself. This self-infatuation is not a marker of a true shepherd and ultimately leads to the demise of the sheep.

I live on a farm, and we have a variety of animals. Two of those animals are sheep. One of them was born with only three legs, so we affectionately named him Tripod. The other sheep is as wide as he is tall. Even after years of having them, I have yet to see a purpose for owning sheep. But I have learned many lessons from being around these sheep. They focus only on what satisfies them, namely water and food. They are so driven by these things that they will sacrifice safety and well being to get what they want. I've noticed these two animals aren't really interested in me unless it's near feeding time. They couldn't care less about me unless I'm bringing them more food.

I'm not surprised that Jesus refers to us as sheep and Himself as the shepherd. Humans and sheep are very much alike, pursuing only the things we think will satisfy. Of course, we are more sophisticated and talk a better game, but the truth is we are in desperate need of a Shepherd—just like sheep.

As shepherds of students, we are accountable to lead them to places of spiritual growth and nourishment. We are to provide safe places for them to hear truth, ask questions, and to understand what it means to "work out [their] own salvation" (Phil. 2:12). This is why we teach with a clear focus on the Word of God. Scripture is what teaches, sustains, convicts, and relates truth to their hearts. It won't be our opinions or best guesses that carry them on difficult days, only God's Word can do that. Sure, there are times when we don't feel needed or even valuable, but that never diminishes the call God has placed on our lives. If you got into student ministry to hear applause for your work and endless thank-yous, you may have chosen the wrong occupation.

We also protect our students spiritually, emotionally, and physically. Guarding against false truths and teaching the Bible allows students to learn what God says. We create spaces for students to learn at their pace and make sure that godly, appropriate leaders are in place to protect them.

How do we grow as shepherds? Clearly it starts with a heart that is sensitive to Jesus. The more time you spend with the Good Shepherd, the more likely you are to be a good shepherd. Here are three other things to consider:

1. **Choose people over process.** The most important aspect of our ministry is the people we serve. Don't get so busy trying to build the Kingdom that you forget to spend time and nurture those around you. Make time with others a priority; put it on the calendar. Have families and groups over to your house so that you don't lose touch with those you serve.

   Ironically, the administrative work of ministry can actually pull us from doing the shepherding work of the ministry. Arrive early to church services and leave late so you can see people and address their needs. Take time to pray for the hurting who are with you. You are the shepherd, and you should smell like your sheep.

2. **Don't use people for what they can do for you.** Shepherds don't take advantage of the sheep. Scripture reminds us that we are to treat everyone well, regardless of what they can do for us (Jas. 2:1). Be careful not to show favoritism to students or families who can do things for you. Love them well, but not to the neglect of others. The students who can do nothing for you probably need the most from you.

▲ PRO TIP

From a friend, Brian Mills: "Walking slowly through the crowds on Sunday will save you time Monday through Saturday."

3. **Interruptions are usually God moments.** Ministry can be busy, no doubt. The 10 days leading up to camp may be responsible for more wrinkles, gray hair, loss of sleep, and weight gain than any other time period in history. (OK. That was a leap, but it's tough!) Shepherding is most often neglected when we are at our busiest. In your efforts to serve people well, don't overlook the opportunity to love them well.

   I'll never forget the first time I was blown off by a minister. An evangelist had come to town and I was so pumped to hear him speak. Four of my friends from another town had committed their lives to Christ after hearing him share the gospel, so I couldn't wait to thank him. When I finally had a chance to speak to him, I quickly shared that I was so grateful for how God was using him. He barely looked my way, simply replied, "Oh," and then walked off.

   I get it. He didn't owe me anything. He was a big timer and probably heard that a lot. But for a young believer who was being called to student ministry, that reply stung. In the moment, I was actually disgusted. I'm not sure all of my bad words had been redeemed out of my mouth yet, but it was a struggle. His response motivated me in that moment to always do my best to make people feel acknowledged and cared for. I've failed some, but I continue to try. We are never too important, too busy, or so in demand that we don't have time for people. Shepherds are different; our sheep are the focus.

SHEPHERDING OURSELVES

Shepherds must be keenly aware of their own struggles. It's difficult to guide and minister to others when you are hurting. There are many in student ministry who need to be ministered to before they can continue to minister to others. Many of the hurting will not seek help, but rather burn out or implode with a scandal of some sort.

Ministry leaders must learn to practice self-care. Honestly, a few years ago if you mentioned "self-care" to me, I would quickly think of it as a weakness. "Be tougher. Push harder. Do the work." Man, was I wrong. I've never been more ashamed for having a machismo, misguided, and self serving attitude. Today, I encourage everyone to see a counselor and get the help they need.

In recent years, two pastors I have known took their own lives. These guys knew the answers and had the resources available to them, but still something was missing. Ministry is demanding and difficult at times, which is why our personal development is a must. To lead others well, being emotionally healthy is an absolute necessity. In his book, *Emotionally Healthy Spirituality*, Pete Scazzero says, "emotional health and spiritual maturity are inseparable. It is not possible to be spiritually mature while remaining emotionally immature."[2]

The Old Testament prophet, Elijah, gives us some insight into the ups and downs of ministry. In 1 Kings 18, he had great success and was completely overjoyed. Fire came from heaven and he defeated his enemies! That's a great day. Elijah was on a mountain top of emotion and ready to conquer the world. And yet, in the very next chapter we find him in the valley of despair, having suffered a great defeat and in the middle of a season of depression. He actually prayed he would die (1 Kings 19:4)!

Like Elijah, many reading this book have experienced difficulty, setbacks, discouragement, and disillusionment. Some people may argue that if you have the right theology or a "strong enough" relationship with Jesus, then depression would never happen. But that's not true. Numerous genuine, God-loving people have suffered from depression. In fact, we find a number of people who experienced seasons of depression in Scripture.

This part of the book on mental health is not exhaustive and is not intended as such. Hopefully it awakens you to—or reminds you of—the reality that we are broken human beings who need the healing of a Great Physician and the care of the Good Shepherd. I'm not a counselor or a clinician, but I want to share a few things that have helped me.

REJECT TOXIC THOUGHTS

Anxiety and depression aren't just present when life is tough. Like Elijah, you can feel depressed even when life is going well. Elijah had a strong relationship with God and was being used by God in very public ways. It's tough to imagine why he would struggle the day after such an amazing victory.

The enemy is the "father of lies" (John 8:44). He asks more questions than he gives answers. In the garden of Eden, He whispered question after question, planting doubt in the newly formed couple's minds. He's a liar, and he hates us because we are made in the image of the one true God.

Reject the lies you hear in your head. Sometimes, when you're right in the middle of a season of depression, the negative thoughts don't seem like lies. So, cling to the truth of God's Word. Separate what you hear and what God says is true about you. And when it's still difficult to recognize a toxic thought for what it is, speak it aloud, write it down, or ask a trusted friend. Doing this gets the lie out of your head— makes it real—and can help you see it more clearly. For some, there will be much more needed than this, but stopping lies at their start helps us keep perspective.

DON'T NEGLECT YOUR PHYSICAL HEALTH

Whether you enjoy running, hiking, or going to the gym—it's good for your overall health when you're active. Consider the effects of your physical body on your mind. Your brain directs your thoughts and muscle movement, helps you reason, contains your memories, keeps you (physically) balanced, regulates your emotions, and much more. Consider your mind's connection to your body, then.

Elijah's situation reminds us of the simplicity of caring for ourselves. After Elijah ran from Jezebel, he fell asleep under a tree, and an angel awakened him and told him to eat. No deep seeded truth, no insights, just, "wake up and eat something." I'm not downplaying the situation, but our physical well-being is tied to our emotional well-being.

To keep your brain and body—and therefore, your emotions—healthy, here are a few tips.

>> **Get consistent sleep as much as possible.**
>> **Eat things that promote your health instead of stealing it from you.**

» **Drink plenty of water.**
» **Get outside and make your body move.**
» **Spend time with the people you love.**

Too simplistic? Maybe. But you get the idea. If you lack sleep, eat a consistently unhealthy diet, exist on coffee and soda, don't exercise, and spend your days without making time for the people you love—it will 100 percent affect the way you feel emotionally. I know that when I am tired and stressed out, my capacity decreases. I'm not as patient as I should be, I get overwhelmed, and I care far less about others' needs because I am consumed with myself.

Ministry is stressful and demands the best from us. Burning a candle at both ends will last for a while, but soon burns out. We can't give our best and navigate the everyday pressures of ministry when we're physically exhausted.

SHARE YOUR STRUGGLES

Pride drives us into isolation and humility leads us to insulation. The fear of being honest keeps many people quiet and drowning in their emotions. My friend, Sarah, has struggled with anxiety and depression for years. She serves on a church staff, is loved by her team, and does an excellent job in her role. It's clear she loves the Lord and her family well.

A few years ago, after two incredible weeks of back-to-back summer camps, Sarah was depressed and wanted to die. She began considering ways to take her own life. She felt alone and feared telling others about her feelings. She wondered if she would lose her job if she talked and what people might say about her.

In spite of her fears, she went to church, found a friend, and shared her feelings. That friend immediately walked alongside Sarah to get help, and Sarah began receiving treatment. After finishing the program, she slowly began to step back into her life. It wasn't easy, and there were setbacks, but she refused to quit. Sarah is thriving today. Her life isn't perfect by any means, but she isn't who she used to be. She shared her feelings and got the help she needed to move forward and not believe the lie that she was alone in her struggles.

You may not have a story like Sarah's, but maybe you do. Either way, if you're struggling with depression or suicidal thoughts, find someone you trust and get the help you need. See a counselor, check into a clinic, or just trust a friend. It feels like a giant weight has been lifted from your shoulders when you can be honest about what you are experiencing.

Being a shepherd and a leader are two sides of the same coin. We must care for our people well, but also organize and lead with growing capacity. I love how Scripture describes David: "He shepherded them with a pure heart and guided them with his skillful hands" (Ps. 78:72). David was a shepherd and a leader. We see that through the way he lived. Let's be the type of ministers who shepherd and lead well.

You don't just wake up one day and become a good leader. Personal growth, commitment to learning, and emotional intelligence are all part of the training. Anyone can be a bad leader—no doubt you've experienced someone who couldn't lead well. Leading well takes discipline and consistency.

Godly leaders are set apart because they want other people to succeed rather than only looking for their own success. The moment you think leadership is all about you is when you begin to use people instead of serving them. Great leaders keep the people they serve ahead of themselves.

Don't confuse having a title with being a leader. It's easy to spot someone who is content with having a title but isn't committed to leading well. They are often unorganized, wait until the last minute to plan, and are okay with just keeping status quo. Their ministry tenure is usually short, and they move on to the next place after their usual "go tos" run out.

In 2006, eight of us sat around a conference room table with great anticipation. In the last year, our church had grown from one campus to two, and within the next few months, we would grow to five campuses. We were talking strategy and planning, with each department leader sharing insights about the upcoming launches. Opening three campuses within a few months of each other is not recommended. There were many details to work out, but becoming a church of five campuses highlighted our greatest need: good leadership.

Eric, our executive pastor at the time, began to challenge each of us about our own development as leaders. Leadership at five campuses would require more from us. He told us, "this growth is going to require each of you to grow and change to lead at a significantly higher level. And truthfully, some of you aren't going to make the leap." *Whoa.* Those words hung in the air for what seemed like an hour. This was a strong challenge to keep growing as leaders or be prepared to step off the team. In that moment, I resolved that I would do whatever it took to grow and lead to the best of my ability.

There is a leadership deficit in student ministry and the change begins with you. This conversation isn't about position, title, or how many students attend your ministry, but rather how will you develop yourself into the leader that God is calling you to be. Like free diving, development doesn't happen overnight. You don't jump into the deep end of leadership and hold your breath for six minutes without trying. Growth takes time and patience.

TO LEAD WELL, YOU HAVE TO KNOW YOURSELF

On the TV show *American Idol*, the first few weeks of the season were always the most interesting to me. If you have seen it, then you know what I am talking about: the audition days. These early episodes were crafted intentionally. Several talented singers would be on the episode along with many who didn't have a chance. I'm not a judge by any means, but it's easy to tell when someone can't sing.

What always blew my mind were the people who proudly described their singing ability, yet when it came time to sing, sounded as though they may have been in physical pain. Inevitably, the performance also caused a type of pain for the listener. When the judges told them, "I'm sorry, you aren't going through to the next round," they were shocked. They often responded with something like, "My mom has always told me I can sing." The judges would gaze incredulously at the contestant—clearly there was a disconnect for this person. They might have a winning personality, but absolutely no vocal talent. It's interesting how people could be so unaware of themselves, especially in front of a national television audience.

Leaders in ministry often make this same mistake. They may be full of personality and charisma, but their lack of self-awareness is painfully obvious. Sometimes leaders think they are relational, but in reality they dominate conversations and often "relate" by sharing "I can one up you" stories.

What about you? How well do you know yourself? It's imperative that leaders understand and are comfortable with who they are so they can effectively lead others. Part of knowing yourself well is knowing the specific ways God has gifted you. God has given you a set of spiritual tools that will assist you in carrying out the plan God has for your life. Take a look at what the apostle Paul said in his letter to the Romans.

According to the grace given to us, we have different gifts: If prophecy, use it according to the proportion of one's faith; if service, use it in service; if teaching, in teaching; if exhorting, in exhortation; giving, with generosity; leading, with diligence; showing mercy, with cheerfulness.
ROMANS 12:6-8

Knowing and using the gifts God has given you helps build up the church, encourage others, and brings comfort by showing others how God can use them. Whether you're new to student ministry or have been serving for years, you might have clarity on what your spiritual gifts are. Although spiritual gifts inventories and personality profiles can't define you or tell you all there is to know about yourself, they can be useful tools in helping you understand your motivations and giftedness.

The Enneagram is one good tool to help you understand your motivations. When I first heard about the Enneagram, I thought, "I don't need to do that. I've done SHAPE, the Berkman profile, DISC—all of that. I think it's a hipster thing." I was wrong! Your Enneagram type or number doesn't define who you are; it exposes who you think you need to be. (Read that last sentence one more time.) The Enneagram can help us heal because it makes us aware of our motivations and feelings. Our emotions are incredibly influential, but we are often unaware of how they affect us. Learning why we behave the way we do is an important step to leading others well, and understanding someone else's behavior and motivation allows us to lead them more effectively.

Think about how you currently evaluate your strengths and weaknesses in a leadership context. Then ask yourself the following questions:

>> **What would you say are your top three strengths?**
>> **What are your two biggest weaknesses?**
>> **Where do you excel?**
>> **Where do you need help?**

If you haven't done so already, identify these areas of strength and weakness, and write them down. Consider how your ministry has been affected both positively and negatively by these tendencies. Evaluate what changes need to be made and who can help you. Then, take your list to a trusted mentor for feedback and see if they agree with your self-assessment. Doing this can not only help you in your first 100 days in student ministry, but the years and years that follow.

When we are aware of who we are, why we behave the way we do, and where we excel, we can thrive as leaders. It is not sinful to want to be a great leader and maximize the opportunity God has given you. Leadership becomes dark and deadly when the focus is on placing yourself in the spotlight instead of Jesus. Be the best at what you do as a means to glorify Christ.

GROWING AS A PROFESSIONAL IN STUDENT MINISTRY.

We don't often hear the words "professional" and "student ministry" in the same sentence. For many, student ministry has been the wild west of the church, associated with little planning and poor communication. Maybe this isn't true at your church, but you probably know of others who fit this description.

To grow as a professional, it's important to consider ways you can grow that will influence the way you serve in the church and in your home. Growing in ministry means not only thriving at work, but winning at home too.

TAKE YOUR PERSONAL GROWTH SERIOUSLY.

Our spiritual growth is paramount to other aspects of life. We know that if we aren't growing in our relationship with God, it's difficult to lead others to grow. Because we believe it's important, we make time to spend reading Scripture, journaling, and learning from the Word. We make room for silence and being quiet before the Lord to hear from Him. We put time and effort into growing spiritual and growing our relationship with God.

Developing ourselves as leaders takes a similar commitment. You will not grow in an area that you aren't disciplined to pursue. I've seen people who are natural athletes but not really great at a sport because they didn't practice the game. It's cool if you can jump out of the gym with your vertical leap, but if you can't dribble or shoot, then you aren't a basketball player. Learning and applying skills will help you develop.

SLOW DOWN AND STEP BACK

Don't confuse being busy with growth. It's strange how culture celebrates living a frantic lifestyle. It feels like a race to see who is most busy, most accomplished, and seemingly getting things done all the time. In this context, social media is an easy place to build a persona that probably doesn't exist. When I see hashtags like, #teamnosleep, I'm not inspired to work harder or shamed into performing more. Rather, it's a clear indication this person isn't capable of managing their time. Could it be that the need for attention is hopelessly trying to fill the gap of actual growth?

As Regan Bach, a consultant and executive coach, said, "One of the biggest fallacies that exists today is the belief that *motion equals progress*."[3] Simply put, being busy doesn't make you better or more effective. However, busyness can reveal the lack of desire or intentionality to grow. So, take the time to improve your leadership. Consider scheduling some "white space" into your calendar. Bach defines white space as "dedicated time, preferably scheduled into your calendar in advance, intended to allow (and sometimes force) you to zoom out, reflect, come up for air, relax, and refuel."[4]

Allowing time to view your development and ministry from the 30,000 foot view will give you a good perspective on what needs to change and how to move forward.

SET GOALS AND ACHIEVE THEM

It isn't sinful to want excel in the area that God has called you. Having a plan to accomplish what needs to be done does not remove God from the equation, but rather creates space for us to narrow our focus. So, consider using a Ministry Action Plan that allows you to set strategic goals and make plans to complete them. (See page 155.) It's easy to set goals, but takes discipline to determine the how and the when of the goal being met.

Setting goals should not be a "shot in the dark" activity. In other words, don't just grasp at a few things you would like to see happen. Consider the strengths, weaknesses, opportunities, and threats to your ministry as a way to evaluate what needs to be done, and then set goals accordingly. Consider these two examples based on a weakness and an opportunity.

> » **Having enough volunteer leaders is a weakness in your ministry.** You need 10 more for student worship. Identifying this specific weakness allows for specific goal setting.
> » **Now, flip the script to a good opportunity.** Your church is surrounded by schools. This is a clear ministry opportunity. A great goal would be to create a plan and put it in place to reach and serve those schools.

Set goals that line up with the actual context of your ministry, not based on what others are doing or how you saw in done in your student ministry growing up.

HAVE A LEGIT WORK ETHIC

Strive to be the most diligent worker in the room and someone who follows through. Choose not to give up when work gets tough or when you don't have answers. Speak life and encouragement to those who serve with you. Set the example for what work looks like in your context.

Notice I didn't say "overwork." Use the hours you have been assigned to accomplish your tasks. I challenge the teams I serve to evaluate their weeks hour by hour. How much time is spent in meetings? In schools? In preparation?

Most of the time, they find hours they didn't know they had. Office life and distractions consume far more time than you often realize.

Diligent work is a stewardship issue. While the work of ministry is never done, completing what's necessary in a timely manner affords other times of rest and solitude. If life is crazy for you now, stop and evaluate how your time is being spent and where. Most often, you will find time you didn't know you had.

PRACTICAL WAYS TO DEVELOP YOURSELF

I loved learning about student ministry in college. My professors were incredible people who loved Jesus and enjoyed serving students. I can still remember one of my professors, Troy Temple, standing on the lectern in our classroom and talking about integrity being weaved into every fiber of our character. It was powerful. I heard countless lessons about organization and church life, but some of my greatest lessons came after graduation while doing the work of the ministry.

Here are a few things that have helped me grow as a leader.

1. **You can learn leadership from anyone.** I've learned leadership from some incredible men and women over the years. Sometimes, those lessons were actually taught to me. However, many of them were caught by me. I try to keep a few leaders that I respect greatly in my circle of friends and learn by watching and listening.

   Tony Isaacs, the first pastor to ever disciple me, taught me much about the Word and ministry. I would say that I learned more by watching his life than what I heard him teach me. I saw how he treated his family and his wife, as well as how he responded to church people who hurt him. Watching him live as a man who loved Jesus affected me deeply. You need to have some guys like Tony around.

   I've also learned from bad leaders. It's easy to see the motives of bad leaders. They are concerned with success for themselves and want you to know they are important. They will use and mistreat people to complete their agenda. But the great leaders I've been around always made me feel like I was important. They told me they believed in me and pushed me to better myself. Truly great leaders make the people around them great—they bring others on the journey.

2. **Don't Get Stuck in the Past.** When ministry leaders do not grow in their craft and awareness, things can be uncomfortable and awkward. Don't be afraid to move forward. Learning from the good—and the bad—in your past doesn't mean you repeat it. Don't sabotage your potential because you haven't grown or learned to communicate your ideas.

   No doubt you have heard the phrases, "leaders are learners" and "leaders are readers." Regardless of how cliche they sound, they are true. Leaders continually push themselves to grow. Reading good books about a variety of topics will help you learn. If reading is tough for you, then join an audio book service or see if your local library has an audio book service. I like to listen to books while driving or mowing the lawn—it's a great use of time! Podcasts are also a solid avenue for growth and learning.

   You can also listen by giving others permission to speak into your life. Ask people you trust to evaluate things you say and do and to hold you accountable. Creating a feedback loop of people you trust to speak truth to you will help you grow and learn emotional awareness.

3. **Evaluate often.** I received a ticket in the mail for running a red light. I instantly thought it was a mistake and prepared my defense. I noticed on the ticket a website where I could view my indiscretion. Still in disbelief, I clicked and watched embarrassingly as the video showed me approaching the red light, slow *almost* to a stop, then turn right. The evidence was there; I am the chief of sinners. My only response was to give my bank info and pay the ticket.

   Evaluation affords us the opportunity to improve what we do. Take time to review past conversations, what was said, and how you said it. Consider how meetings were conducted, how your time was spent, and gather others to break down activities or events that have taken place. After events, like camp, our student team will gather and review how the week went. Each person on the team is expected to come ready to discuss what went right, what went wrong, and new possibilities. We also ask key volunteers for their insight. A great evaluation time should make you and the ministry better.

Growth is never easy. If it was, everyone would do it. Start in the shallow end of the pool, and work on the leadership disciplines required to take you deeper. Before long, you will see your capacity for ministry and leadership begin to grow.

›› QUESTIONS

1. Name someone who has shepherded you well. What was significant about how that person cared for you?

_____

_____

_____

_____

_____

2. How would you rate your shepherding skills? What can be improved?

_____

_____

_____

_____

_____

3. Name a few of your best practices for developing yourself as a leader. Then, name one practice you'd like to add.

_____

_____

_____

_____

_____

4. Why is it a mistake to confuse being busy with being a great leader? How have you seen this to be true in your life?

_____

_____

_____

_____

_____

PART
TWO

LEADING AND DEVELOPING OTHERS

"When a leader is ablaze with passion, people invariably are attracted to the flame."[1]

JOHN MAXWELL

OUR FAMILY LOVES THE FLORIDA KEYS. When we lived in Miami, it was normal to drive to the Keys for the evening and enjoy dinner while watching the sunset. As a result, we found a few favorite restaurants that we still visit when we return on vacation. Last fall, we visited Sundowner's, one of our favorites in Key Largo. We were sitting near the water, enjoying the sunset and listening to live music. The band on stage was pretty good, and they were playing familiar songs that had the crowd singing along.

Then I noticed something strange. The lead singer was definitely singing, but her attention and focus were somewhere else entirely. During the songs, she would flip scroll through social media on her tablet while singing! It was so strange. Hundreds of people were dialed into her voice, but clearly, checking her social media account was more important. At that point, I lost interest in the band. You can't possibly sing "Don't Stop Believing" by Journey and not be completely committed to the song! How in the world do you listen to someone who doesn't believe or get into what she is singing?

Fortunately, a disillusioned cover band only impacts one evening. When it comes to leadership, a person who is disconnected from the vision can cause catastrophic issues. The only people who follow unclear leaders are people who are unsure about themselves.

A few years into my journey as a leader, I heard Andy Stanley speak about leadership at the Catalyst Conference. He said, "Leadership is stewardship, it's temporary, and you're accountable."[2] The longer I'm in ministry, the more profound those words become. How we manage budgets, time, resources, and people are an incredible responsibility. Even if you are in the same role for 40 years, it's temporary in light of eternity. We are accountable for what we have taught and how we have shepherded our people.

Leadership is far more than a position—it's an action that calls other people to join the journey. It is not a position to be attained, but an opportunity to guide a movement. Yet, there are numerous definitions for leadership out there. To narrow it down, let's define what leadership looks like in student ministry.

LEADERSHIP IS INFLUENCE

When most people think or talk about leadership, the emphasis is usually on the authority someone has over other people. Culture celebrates people of power and romanticizes the idea of being a "boss." The true beauty of leadership isn't finding satisfaction in telling others what to do, but rather raising up other people to serve alongside you. Great leaders see value in others and in helping them reach the potential that God has given them. As ministry leaders, it's our responsibility to help others discover and learn how to live out the calling God has given them.

If you are now or have ever been part of a church that expects the pastoral staff to do everything, then you understand where this conversation is going. In many churches, the pastor, student pastor, or worship pastor are expected to carry the entire ministry workload. Student pastors are expected to teach, hang with students, run the church website (no matter how antiquated it is), operate the church's social media, be the fill in sound/audio person, and do announcements. Oh, don't forget hospital visits, set up and tear down, janitorial help when needed, cutting the church grass, going to funerals, and attending every meeting. Let's also include speaking to the adult service on key holiday weekends like July 4th and New Years. (But, let's be honest, we're happy speak any chance we get!)

Why can't the student pastor do all of this? They get a paychecks, get to go on paid vacations every summer (camp), visit exotic locations (mission trips), and only work one day a week! (Obviously I'm being sarcastic!) Even if it's not the expectation of others at church, our own longing to find approval drives us to busyness. The truth is that God's plan for church leadership isn't for us to be overwhelmingly busy, but rather we are to equip the saints to do the work of the ministry. Being busy isn't a sign of progress and its rarely a sign of good leadership. If leadership is influence, then our measure of success isn't as much what we accomplish as it is who we develop.

PRO TIP

You must get things done. However, when you lead and train others to walk with you, much more can be done than you could ever accomplish alone.

Influence plays a primary role in whether or not people will follow our leadership. We must be credible and believable to the people around us. Influence translates into people trusting you and following the direction you are leading. They are willing to follow you as you follow Christ. Influence is also important for others to grow. They will allow themselves to be taught and discipled when you have shown them why it matters. Look at what Ephesians 4 says about the important of influence.

And he himself gave some to be apostles, some prophets, some evangelists, some pastors and teachers, to equip the saints for the work of ministry, to build up the body of Christ, until we all reach unity in the faith and in the knowledge of God's Son, growing into maturity with a stature measured by Christ's fullness. Then we will no longer be little children, tossed by the waves and blown around by every wind of teaching, by human cunning with cleverness in the techniques of deceit. But speaking the truth in love, let us grow in every way into him who is the head—Christ. From him the whole body, fitted and knit together by every supporting ligament, promotes the growth of the body for building itself up in love by the proper working of each individual part.

EPHESIANS 4:11-16

To summarize, Ephesians 4 says that the ministry leaders' primary responsibility isn't just to work, but to develop others to do the work. So, let's explore the idea of leading others. How do you lead other people when you aren't giving them a paycheck? What qualities make a leader credible and believable?

"Your title makes you a manager.
Your people make you a leader."[3]
DONNA DUBINSKY

You are only a leader if others are willing to follow in the direction you're headed. Since being a dictator isn't a biblically sustainable model in church ministry, great leadership is predicated on the type of person you are. The following list of qualities that people will follow is not exhaustive, but it's understood that true leadership begins at the feet of Jesus. Trying to lead people to serve God while only serving yourself is disastrous. Love the Lord your God, love others, and hone these characteristics in your life.

HUMILITY

Humility is often twisted and perceived as a sense of unworthiness or some strange version of self-loathing. Neither one of those ideas are true. As Rick Warren said, "Humility is not thinking less of yourself; it is thinking of yourself less."[4] Translation: humility is understanding that you don't have to be the center of every story and a genuine desire to see other people win.

Culture takes a strange approach to humility. On social media, people will be semitransparent about an issue they want to discuss and seem to be humble. But in their attempt to appear humble, they are really just drawing attention to themselves by sharing just enough to garner what they are seeking. It's easy to be humble when you serve others—as long as you record it and post it later for everyone to see your good deeds.

Humility doesn't need the attention or to always be right and it doesn't make you feel compelled to manipulate others into thinking you are something that you're not. True humility hits differently, and students recognize it. Volunteers crave humility in a leader. Paul gave clear instruction as to how we should approach ourselves and others.

Do nothing out of selfish ambition or conceit, but in humility consider others as more important than yourselves. Everyone should look not to his own interests, but rather to the interests of others.
PHILIPPIANS 2:3-4

Leadership in the church requires humility. Our job is to serve others; that's our calling. It's hard to serve others and serve yourself at the same time. If you expect to be respected because of a title, you've missed what it means to have humility.

TRUSTWORTHINESS

If you're trustworthy, the people you serve can confidently follow your lead. When there is a lack of confidence, the ministry suffers. Even the most ardent of volunteers are hesitant when the person leading them isn't honest.

Do what you say you will do to the best of your ability. Don't make plans and promises with no intention of following through. If you lose credibility with those you lead, it will be very difficult to move the ministry forward. When you make a mistake, a sincere apology and plan for moving forward are far more valuable than sorry excuses. Just like a good front woman for a band engages with what she's singing, a leader embraces the truth.

Live out the vision of what you say is important. If it's important to have a daily quiet time, be sure that's true for you as much as it is for them. Sharing your faith, being a wise steward of your money, and loving your neighbor are all scriptural—and part of what we teach our students. It's right for us to do these things even if we don't plan to use them in a sermon illustration. You are trustworthy when you embrace and live out all the things you say are true.

INTENTIONALITY

Being purposeful and intentional in relationships means two things: the leader is actually focused on what is being said to them, rather than mentally drifting off toward the next responsibility. And when the leader is clearly giving their full attention, the other person in the conversation knows that they have value. The leader shows she isn't too busy or distracted to care for the individual.

» **Develop ways to remember people's names and what they share in common with you.** If someone asks you to pray for something specific, pull out your phone and make a note immediately. There are two wins in doing this: you remember to pray and they believe you are actually going to do it. We Christians are often far more eager to tell others we will pray for them but lack the discipline to do it.

» **Discipline yourself to reduce how often you look at your phone.** If, as the leader, you seem to care more about what's happening outside the room, it will be assumed you don't have time for the people in front of you.

Not long ago I was in South Carolina spending time with some of the leadership team of a large, multi-site church. My friend Collin and I spent several hours with one particular lead team member, asking questions and learning more about their systems and processes. About two hours into the conversation, I realized he had never checked his phone—not one pick up or even a glance. So I continued to watch and see: He never once picked up his phone in four hours. I couldn't believe it! This guy has an insane amount of responsibilities at the church and is always in demand. Yet, he made our group feel as though nothing else mattered. That's intentionality.

Developing focus to make individuals feel important is a discipline that needs constant practice. Have you ever felt like you weren't valued because someone didn't have time for you? Or had a conversation with someone who was there physically but was clearly distracted and seemingly disconnected from the conversation? As leaders, we must do our best to keep our people from feeling that way. Conversations and interruptions are not a disruption to our ministry, they are our ministry.

» **Value others for who they are, not for what they can do for you or your ministry.** When people matter for who they are, value is given. If they are only appreciated for what they contribute, value is actually taken from them. People want to follow leaders who add value to their life. Truth: you want to follow leaders who add value to you.

I struggled at one point in my ministry when I was working for someone who only valued what I could contribute. Obviously this was never spoken, but the effects were painfully loud. There was no relationship or development, only expectation that I would bring my best to the table each day regardless of the circumstances. When the phone rang and the caller ID showed who it was, I knew there was work to be done.

When the focus is only on what is accomplished, the true heart of the leader is revealed. A ministry led with this mindset will create disgruntled, burned-out volunteers who will question why it's important to serve if no one cares about them.

GENEROSITY

Your generosity encourages others to be generous. Spend time with your leaders and volunteers. Schedule lunches, coffees, and dinners at your home. Remember, how you share your time with leaders sets an example of how they should spend time with students.

Give your leaders the best you can afford. That's a sliding scale—everyone's budget is different. But what I've found to be true over the years from leaders and volunteers is that it's not about how much money went into a thing but the thought. In Miami, we didn't have a large budget for leader gifts. So, we asked one of our pastors—who is an expert with a smoker—to cook for a party.

Gifts were minimal—so minimal that it was actually tiny plastic trophies. However, each trophy was accompanied by a certificate that was a specific, true characteristic of that person. The "blinker Dan award" was the guy most likely to leave a church bus blinker on for miles. The "mama Kim" award went to a woman who made sure the students were always fed well. Not all of them were funny, but each one was sincere. It doesn't take a large bank account for your leaders to understand that you know and see them.

Becoming a leader worth following is not a destination; it's a continual journey of becoming. When you are a leader worth following, be sure you are intentional with how you develop the people who follow you.

WORDS CREATE WORLDS

How we speak creates the culture we live in. If you encourage, others will be uplifted and encourage others also. If you speak negatively, cast doubt, and are cynical, those who follow you will do the same. Consider what the Book of James says about the power of the tongue.

> *With the tongue we bless our Lord and Father, and with it we curse people who are made in God's likeness. Blessing and cursing come out of the same mouth. My brothers and sisters, these things should not be this way.*
> **JAMES 3:9-10**

I've always believed that words were powerful, but what I witnessed one afternoon affirmed this truth for me. Our church was hosting the funeral for a family of four. Two of the deceased were teen girls who attend our ministry and were in my wife's class at a local middle school. The situation was horrific. The father of the family shot and killed his two daughters, his wife, and then himself.

During the funeral, all four caskets were at the front. The despair in the room was far heavier than normal funerals, like an unspoken condemnation of the horror that had been committed. Different family members got up to speak and share memories; not one person mentioned the father even though it was his service also. That is until Naomi began to speak. Naomi was the niece of the dad, the perpetrator of the crimes. She lived with the family usually and was away at school during the tragedy. She addressed the mom, and then each daughter, like everyone else had done. Then she paused.

"Uncle," she said, "I miss you, I love you, and I forgive you."

The crowd of over 2000 people broke into tears. It felt like a dam holding back the emotional floodwaters had broken and all the feelings were released. After a few moments, the room changed. It was a sad situation, but Naomi's words helped to lift the unbearable weight. Naomi chose to speak life when it would have made sense to speak hate. She spoke love when no one expected her to do so, and it changed everything.

Speak life into those around you and build them up. You don't have to lie and sugarcoat, but don't focus on the negative. Choose to find the good in situations and highlight what is right. Make sure the world you create with your words is one that you would want to live in and can see others thrive in.

DEVELOPING OTHERS

If recruiting, training, and raising up great volunteer leaders was easy, every student ministry in the world would be fully staffed with loving, engaged, and qualified volunteer leaders. The truth is, it's not easy. Simply acknowledging the need for trained leaders isn't enough. A student ministry must have focused and organized development for volunteer leaders to be recruited and trained well.

BARRIERS

We must ask and answer some honest questions about the barriers that keep us from training leaders well. Here are a few reasons ministry leaders aren't raising up the next wave of trained volunteers.

1. **Our ego.** "I want the credit for the success." This is the idea that if you plan, perform, and complete what needs to be done, then everyone will applaud your actions. Often, developing others does not happen because our pride demands that we handle everything on our own. A word of caution: this can be disguised behind phrases like, "I'm just a hard worker." Don't believe your own hype.

2. **Expediency.** I once saw a sign that said, "If you want to go fast, go alone. If you want to go farther, take someone with you." I thought of leadership immediately. Of course it's faster if you do things on your own, but thats not leadership—that's "doership." If this is how you lead, then you probably get easily frustrated with others and see them as an inconvenience. John Maxwell, author and leadership guru, would say that you are the "lid" to your ministry. It can't grow and become all that God has for it because you aren't willing to invest in others.[5]

3. **Excellence.** "It will be better if I do it." You've probably heard the statement, "If you want it done right, you have to do it yourself." That's absolutely true for those who don't know how to develop others. There will definitely be a learning curve when something new is introduced, but when you train well, someone else can do it too. Consider this: if a leader can do something 80 percent as well as you, it is good enough. Continue to train them to 100 percent, but give them room to learn.

4. **Control.** "I can't control it if someone else is doing it." Great leaders have learned how to give away ministry to others and loosen the grip of micromanaging. Your capacity as a leader will be the limit to your ministry if control is defining your leadership.

   We are afraid of things we can't control in student ministry. We like things in one room, at one location, where it's easy to keep eyes on everyone. Too many variables make us uncomfortable. It's easier to horde authority and keep the notion of "control" than it is to raise up leaders and delegate responsibility. But raising up and developing leaders expands our influence and gives others opportunity to live out what God has called them to do. Training well reduces the panic of letting go of control.

RECRUITING VOLUNTEERS

After you have worked through the barriers that hinder you from engaging others, develop your recruiting style. Recruitment of volunteers is not for the faint of heart—it takes courage, persistence, and an unshakable belief in what God has called you to do.

Student ministry volunteers are some of the most incredible people on the planet. Choosing to take their personal time and invest in the lives of students is incredibly sacrificial. We all know it can be difficult to find the right volunteers, but it's a worthwhile struggle.

In my experience, about one in five adults who are asked to serve show interest and take the next step. Many people will be quick to sign up on a list after an announcement, but until they are willing to walk through the onboarding process (including background checks), it doesn't amount to much. Be sure to follow up with the interested people, but don't stop recruiting in the meantime.

Whether you realize it or not, the volunteers you have now or hope to recruit are largely dependent on you. It's easy to complain about people in the church not being motivated, but we first need to look at ourselves, who we are, and how we recruit. How you present yourself and the ministry are important. Be sure you can articulate your vision for the ministry clearly. Tell volunteers why student ministry is important, what's the point of serving, and how their contribution can help make the vision of your church's student ministry a reality.

Take the time to develop two recruitment talks. One should be about 20 seconds in length and articulate why serving in student ministry matters. This way, you can have a prepared but brief statement while on the go. The other talk should be about two minutes long—not 10 minutes—and share more without being overwhelming. If your talks are prepared well, the purpose of student ministry will be clear, and you will be perceived as someone who is passionate about what they do.

It's important for potential volunteers to know what they are signing up for. They want to know how they fit and if their gifts can be used. They want to know what will be expected of them and whether or not they have what it takes to do what you're asking. These are all important ideas to keep in mind. This being said, don't just recruit people because they have a pulse. Find the right people and place them in the right spots.

Jovanni was a senior in high school and interested in ministry. He served in a few capacities and did well, so we put him in charge of the greeters for our high school ministry's Saturday night service. His responsibility was to recruit other students and train them to greet as other students came to the service.

One Saturday night, I was across campus and came to see how Jovanni was doing. All the greeters were in place and welcoming people as they came in. However, there was one small issue. With the best of intentions, Jovanni had recruited some kids from his high school to greet with him. Two of the first greeters I saw were about six feet tall and covered in tattoos. The third greeter was nice, but had a reputation for being a drug dealer (he was) at his school. So, our greeting at that position that night looked like an offense line with a drug problem.

There is no problem with recruiting big guys with tattoos or even engaging drug dealers. But freshman girls attending the service may become intimidated immediately. Guys struggling with the old way of life may try to score a bag on the way to service. Putting the two big guys at different locations and asking the drug dealer to wait to serve would have been a better call. I love each of those kids to this day. But leading requires discernment. Volunteers and students are relying on you. Press on with recruitment. Attract volunteers and lead them well. But be discerning about how your deploy them.

RECRUITMENT STRATEGY

Consider the "how" of recruitment. Why are you recruiting volunteers? Is it to fill the needs you have in ministry or is it to see others empowered to live out the giftedness that God has given them?

Your answer to those questions directly relates your recruitment style. For example, if you are only filling spots on an organizational chart because you have a need, those people will be treated accordingly. Be careful not to use just anybody to fill a ministry need.

In reality, both statements should be true. There are needs to be filled, but the desire is for people to exercise their giftedness by serving. How you communicate this truth to potential volunteers show them the intentionality you have for them. Leaders are drawn to leaders who want to invest in them and develop them.

DELEGATE, DON'T DUMP.

Unless leaders are being intentional with how they develop, they have a tendency to "dump" responsibility on a rising leader. The scenario looks the same, even with seasoned veterans. The leader is consumed with other things but knows that "x" is important. She recruits a volunteer, gives brief instructions, and conveys the importance of what is happening. There are usually a few thoughts on how thankful the leader is that the volunteer is helping out, then she takes her hands off the proverbial wheel. She has effectively dumped the responsibility onto someone else. In this dumping scenario, the leader's heart is disengaged from the work. They aren't concerned with the ultimate responsibility, and any warm bodied person will do.[6] It is irresponsible and negligent to handle ministry this way.

The volunteer is excited at first, eager to execute the recently assigned task well. Soon after, the once excited and hopeful volunteer realizes there's far more to the task than she initially thought, and she becomes discouraged. Disappointment turns into frustration, and the volunteer usually steps away without making a scene. Once in a while, the volunteer will circle back and ask for more clarity, but that's not always the case. They might be embarrassed to admit that they need help so they decide to just stop serving.

This scenario is repeated time and time again in ministry. It's not the volunteer's fault that she was never trained properly, but now her view of serving in ministry is distorted. For most, its difficult to envision serving again, at least in the immediate future. Rather than dumping responsibility onto your volunteers, train well and often.

TRAINING FOR THE FUTURE

Good leadership provides training to raise up new leaders while simultaneously doing ministry. If the work of the ministry is to continue, then consistent development is needed. Here are some helpful tips for effective training.

» **Training content for your leaders should be practical, timely, and give answers to potential problems.** Before creating a planning schedule, first create a list of the topics and issues that need to be addressed.
  » What problems do we have now that need to be addressed?
  » What do our leaders need to know?
  » How do we help them become excellent at what they do?
  » What training can help them win while serving students and while at home?

  Assessing the right information can lead to powerful, helpful meeting times. If the content isn't good or helpful, leaders will not make it a priority to attend. Gather what you need to teach, and then decide how and when to share the information.
» **Plan consistent times of training for your volunteers.** We all know getting leaders to come learn on a Monday night is difficult, so consider how you can use the time they are already at church. If your student programming is on Wednesday night, maybe invite them earlier for training. Or consider Sunday after church as an opportune time. If you strategize your meetings well, you don't need to meet for an hour every time.
» **Use various methods to train leaders.** It's not necessary to meet in person every time. Video calls (since we are all experts now) can afford

opportunities for more leaders to attend. The benefit of video calls is that no one has to leave home, and it's far more convenient.

» **Emails also have their place.** If used wisely, they can be briefly informational and offer resources. A timely email can be very helpful, but an overload of emails becomes a burden.

» **Prerecorded videos can also be helpful.** This way leaders can watch the training when it is convenient for them. Potentially include some follow up questions to be answered and help them engage.

Be the type of leader who lives out what they say. Don't be comfortable saying one thing from stage but being disconnected in the crowd. A loving, shepherding leader who trains and develops well will have no issue producing great leaders.

» QUESTIONS

1. Define leadership in your words.

2. What would you say makes you a leader? How does your leadership influence those around you?

3. What barriers do you face in developing others? How can you overcome them?

4. What is your recruitment strategy? If you never got another stage announcement in "big church," how would you recruit volunteers?

6

HOPE IS NOT A STRATEGY

"Strategy is a commodity, execution is an art."[1]

PETER DRUCKER

SEAWORLD IS AN AMAZING PLACE. When I would visit as a kid, I was blown away by the aerobatic displays and the variety of sea life. One show that stands out in my memory is the Orca presentation. The trainers taught 10,000 pound killer whales to soar out of the water and jump over a rope 20 feet in the air. It blew my mind!

Clearly, Orcas aren't born with the instinct to obey a trainer's whistle and soar into the sky. Although it looks effortless, an incredible amount of training goes into performing one 30 minute show. Before a ticket is ever sold, a trainer saw potential in a particular whale and trained it to do something amazing.

The Orca's love of fish is one of the vital tools the trainers leverage to teach the massive mammal to fly. The process starts slowly. First, the Orca is trained to simply swim over a rope placed above the pool floor. When he does that, he gets a fish. When that becomes familiar, the rope is raised, the process starts over, and he receives another fish. After mastering each rope height, he receives a reward, and the rope is raised. You see a pattern here. The whales don't start at jumping 20 feet in the air, they start by swimming over a rope laying above the floor of the tank. They are gradually and intentionally trained how to jump to new heights.[2] We only see the trained, disciplined whale doing what it was taught to do in the show. It's a time intensive process, but all the training leads to people being willing to wait hours in line and spend hard earned money to see the amazing results.

SEATING CAPACITY

For far too long, student ministry has underestimated the heights to which our students can soar spiritually. We've kept the rope very low and equated spiritual growth with showing up to a program once or twice a week. The figurative rope is laid on the bottom of the pool and we cheer when students "swim" over it. Regrettably, that's the extent of our expectations.

Learning to help students develop spiritual maturity doesn't happen overnight. It's not a six-week Bible study with your best group leader. It won't happen by filling the student ministry calendar with events and options, hoping students become disciple makers. Discipleship is not a drive-through process; it's more like a slow cooker recipe.

For example, one way we lower the standard is by maintaining a seating capacity mindset, where the goal is to fill the seats each week. We should want to fill the seats each week—the more students show up, the greater their opportunity to hear the gospel. But keeping the expectation at just showing up to church brings results that are indicative of where many student ministries are today—a mile wide, but an inch deep.

In a seating capacity mindset what happens in the ministry is determined by whether it will put students in seats. What's measured as a win is a full room, the numbers entered (and maybe even celebrated on social media), students instructed to come back next week and to "bring a friend." That's it; they met their goal. Then, leaders focus on the next week and how to do it all over again.

Listen, getting students to show up is an incredible feat, but if that's the only intent, the goal is short-sighted and the standard is set ridiculously low. There is a real danger with seating-capacity thinking. Students learn by observation more than by what they are told. If we celebrate students when they show up but never show them the next spiritual step, they will believe they are already doing all that's necessary to grow. Without a word being said, students are learning: "Just show up when its your turn and have a great time. You've done all you needed to do to remain spiritually healthy."

Apply this thinking over the course of a few years. If the room is full every week, does that fulfill what Jesus commanded us to do? Can we lay our heads down on our pillows at night and know for certain that we have fulfilled the

Great Commission? Did we do what our Lord commanded by getting students to show up? Even more terrifying, do we pat ourselves on the back because we did at least part of what Jesus said? A seating-capacity mindset robs students of experiencing God more deeply. Shame on us when we are comfortable to let our students swim over a rope in the spiritual shallow end when they are capable of what God has intended for them, leaping over the rope 20 feet in the air.

SENDING CAPACITY

Discipleship is intentionally and consistently raising the standard for students to grow spiritually. Discipling means challenging and showing students how to grow in their relationship with Christ. You may have read the paragraphs above and thought, "Wait. It's wrong to fill the room or have big events?" Of course not! But filling the room isn't the point.

A sending-capacity mindset focuses on students gathering and then going. The emphasis moves from what only happens in the building to what happens when students make disciples on their own. When a sending culture is fully in the ministry DNA, students are disciple-makers on their own, without the church telling them to do it. It's important to ask yourself what's happening after students leave the student ministry area.

> » **What does their life look like then?**
> » **Are they pursuing Jesus on their own?**
> » **How do they love their neighbor?**
> » **Has our ministry equipped them to do those things?**

Perspective is important. In 2019, my wife, Jen, and I went with Student Leadership University 301 to Europe. It was an amazing experience. We were able to visit some places we had only dreamed about, and we learned so much more about leadership. Experiencing all of this with some incredible friends made our trip that much more awesome.

Seeing and ascending the Eiffel Tower was memorable. Notice I didn't use the word "climb," but ascend. There was no way, in 106 degree weather, that we were climbing that metal monstrosity. Riding the elevators was a worthwhile experience. While the street view of Paris is cool, it's different than what the movies show. There are a ton of people, and the sidewalks are very busy. The streets aren't very clean, and traffic constantly gets backed up.

Sometimes, it's tough to appreciate the beauty of Paris when you are walking around on the street level. But the view from the top of the Eiffel Tower is vastly different. You can see much of the city and observe how the streets are laid out. Perspective changes everything. So, I want to challenge you to look at your ministry with a "top of the tower" view. Perspective changes how we view what we are doing and why we are doing it. We must be able to see if we are fulfilling *all* of the Great Commission—seeing students become disciples who are disciple-makers.

A BETTER WAY

In 2019, Ben Trueblood, Director of Student Ministry for Lifeway Christian Resources, wrote a book called *Within Reach*. It's a short book that unpacks the alarming reality that 66 percent of students who graduate from high school are stepping out of church.[3] They aren't necessarily leaving their faith but they're leaving the church.

Previous studies on why students are leave the church have been difficult to trust. They are often plagued by vague descriptions and generalities and end up feeling like a shot at student ministry rather than a tool to help us improve. Here are the parameters that make *Within Reach* credible. The data was gathered from thousands of students across the country from coast to coast. Participants were considered "active" in their church if they attended two times or more per month. The study was not denomination specific, but Protestant. Many of those interviewed were involved in serving and/or participating in groups at their church.[4]

The results of this study paint a less than ideal picture. Usually when people in ministry hear how many students are leaving church after high school, they point to forces outside the church as the culprits. Too often, we are reluctant to look at what is happening inside the church. People think, "It's those atheist professors" or "It's that party life at college." Some would even go as far as to say this is an "I hate God now" problem. But the survey results don't show that. Sure, those things could be a factor, but the stark reality is that the lion's share of ownership must be laid at the feet of student ministry.

But this study doesn't leave us without any ideas moving forward. Instead, it actually shows how we can help students. There are clearly defined ways that student ministries can influence a student and help them stay connected to church. According to the research, here are a few of the factors that motivated students to stay in church.

1. **A significant relationship with adults while they are 15-18 years of age.** This is more than a high-five on the way in the door or asking where they've been when they don't show up for a while. This is a significant relationship.

2. **Regularly reading the Bible for themselves before age 18.** These students knew how to navigate the Word of God for themselves and could effectively read and study it alone.

3. **A relationship with the church that helps guide them in everyday decisions.** This is a result of students feeling connected to the church and feeling like they are part of the church.[5]

Fortunately, 66 percent is not a death sentence and can change for the better. Our role as spiritual influencers in students' lives is far greater than just asking them to show up.

WHERE DO WE GO FROM HERE?

Too many of us have often been happy with how we do church while we grow frustrated with the results. We quickly blame the people in the seats but rarely pause to evaluate ourselves and our processes. The first two thoughts on a seating-capacity mindset and students staying in church are not mutually exclusive: We can do better, and we must raise the standard in our own leadership. It's possible that we have been better at connecting students to student ministry than we have been at connecting them to the gospel. Raising the standard for our students doesn't happen "organically."

 SOAPBOX WARNING

"Organic" is a great buzzword but often holds no weight. It almost seems like when there isn't an answer, the phrase, "I think it happens organically," mystically fills in the gaps. Weeds grow in our yards organically and make them look awful. Growing healthy plants organically actually takes great intentionality.

I've always been puzzled by the use of the word *organic* in relationship to ministry. Nothing of value or of great significance happens organically. Discipleship has never happened that way; it must be intentional. Scripture gives us a great example, illustrating the effects of the lack of intentionality.

After these things, the LORD's servant, Joshua son of Nun, died
at the age of 110. They buried him in his allotted territory at
Timnath-serah, in the hill country of Ephraim north of Mount
Gaash. Israel worshiped the LORD throughout Joshua's lifetime
and during the lifetimes of the elders who outlived Joshua and
who had experienced all the works the LORD had done for Israel.
JOSHUA 24:29-31

In these verses, Joshua had passed away. The people that were with Joshua and lived the same experiences, worshiped the Lord until they passed away. But look what the Book of Judges tells us about the people who came after them.

Joshua son of Nun, the servant of the LORD, died at the age
of 110. They buried him in the territory of his inheritance, in
Timnath-heres, in the hill country of Ephraim, north of Mount
Gaash. That whole generation was also gathered to their
ancestors. After them another generation rose up who did not
know the LORD or the works he had done for Israel.
JUDGES 2:8-10

Wait. What? How can that be true? Read those verses again. The generation that was with Joshua worshiped God, but the generation that came after didn't know God or what He had done. Scripture isn't clear on what exactly happened, but it's clear what didn't happen: There were many people who loved God but failed to pass that love on to the next generation. There was a lack of discipleship. Passing on the faith failed to happen organically!

In the Great Commission, Jesus gave clear instruction about what discipleship looks like. Often, the Great Commission is reduced to "go and tell," but there is so much more to it. We must go and tell, but we must also teach and disciple just as fiercely.

Jesus came near and said to them, "All authority has been given to me
in heaven and on earth. Go, therefore, and make disciples of all nations,
baptizing them in the name of the Father and of the Son and of the Holy

Spirit, teaching them to observe everything I have commanded you. And remember, I am with you always, to the end of the age."
MATTHEW 28:18-20

CREATING YOUR DISCIPLESHIP PATHWAY

I live just outside of Nashville, Tennessee, but one of my favorite places in the world is in southern California—a little town called Huntington Beach. I love the surf, the laid back vibe, and the climate. I've always flown to SoCal, because driving there from Tennessee seems to border on insanity. However, if I were to drive, I would most certainly use a GPS app for directions. Disaster would strike if I jumped in my truck and followed the sun while using the compass on my rear view mirror. Hopefully, I would eventually make it to Huntington Beach. Since hope isn't a strategy, though, I will use a proven method.

A discipleship pathway is a spiritual roadmap. It shows students what steps to take to grow spiritually. The pathway consists of environments that are strategically designed to help them grow. At Long Hollow, the church where I serve, this is what the discipleship pathway looks like.

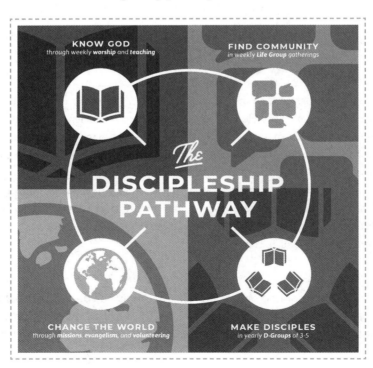

In our ministry, we want students to know God, find community, make disciples, and change the world. That sounds great, but how do we put it into practice? Clearly, we can't just put a slogan on the church website and assume students are growing in their faith. There are programs attached to each step of our pathway. The goal is for each step to lead students to a deeper, more committed walk with Christ.

> » **Know God.** When encouraging students to know God, they are invited to attend a Wednesday night service. It's a large group gathering that includes worship, teaching, and other elements designed to engage students. Wednesdays are also a great environment to invite friends who are new to church. Probably like most youth ministry nights, students learn, meet new friends, and have fun. Students are also given several opportunities to talk with a leader and other students about what they are learning during the teaching.
> » **Find community.** Students engaging in the second step of the pathway are part of a life group (small group). Life groups consist of 10-12 students with two adult leaders. In this environment, discussion is based around the teaching from our Wednesday night service. This allows students to discuss and learn from what they were taught. Life groups provide the opportunity to live in biblical community. They give students opportunity to practice the "one anothers" of the Bible. These groups meet weekly in various places and times.
> » **Make disciples.** The third part of the pathway is the aspect that requires the most commitment. Students are gathered in groups of three to five and are discipled by a leader of the same gender. In a discipleship group or "d-group," students share what God is teaching them weekly, memorize Scripture, live on mission, and agree to accountability. The groups don't grow numerically once they are started because it's tough to have trust and accountability when new faces show up.
> » **Change the world.** The final part of the discipleship pathway challenges students to use their spiritual gifts to serve the body of Christ inside the church and to live missionally outside the church. It isn't required to be in a life group or d-group to serve or live on mission. Serving encompasses everything from being on the student ministry serve team, serving in kids ministry or any other area that is appropriate. Living missionally means loving the community and going on mission trips, and most importantly, loving their neighbors as they love themselves and sharing their faith.

This pathway isn't linear, it's cyclical. Students don't have to attend Wednesday night to engage in another area. Some students come to a life group for the first time or love the community with us in some way. D-groups usually aren't the first place a student attends because those groups don't accept new students once they've started. Each environment has been intentionally placed along the pathway so there is a clear plan for discipleship. Students are consistently encouraged to take more committed steps.

An argument could be made that programs don't spiritually grow students. I would agree wholeheartedly. I've seen students engage in all forms of church activities and still be far from God. Programs do not grow students. We know it's God who does the growing, but we must put ourselves in an environment to grow. For this reason, you have a quiet time or read a devotional in the morning—you know that time is reserved for you and God. The discipline of a specific time and place will not grow you spiritually—an open heart and an open Bible will be the catalyst for your growth. The same is true with programs. When students have a desire to grow in their relationship with God, the program only facilitates that growth.

HOW TO GET STARTED

How do you create a pathway that's unique to your ministry? Consider walking through these three areas with those in your ministry who think strategically. I learn by observing things visually, so I'll illustrate a process in this way:

THEOLOGY » PHILOSOPHY » ACTIONS

» **Theology.** Start by considering theology. Who does God say He is? What are His attributes? We know more about God by what we see in the life of Jesus. Jesus is loving and kind, and He is also just and holy. We read in Scripture that Jesus discipled, lived in community, served others, and loved people who were far from Him. With a firm understanding of who God is because of what is true about Jesus, we can create our philosophy of ministry. The truth of who God is must shape our philosophy of ministry.

» **Philosophy.** A philosophy of ministry is "why" we do what we do. Since we understand what the Bible says is true about God, we know that our ministry philosophy should align with Scripture. For example, Jesus clearly loves lost people. Our ministry philosophy should embrace that. Why do we believe small groups are important? Because Jesus spent much of His time investing in 12 men. They did life together, went to parties together, and even occasionally took a boat ride together. Case in point: our ministry should reflect the person of Jesus and how He did ministry. The church has the mission to help people become more like Jesus, and the pathway provides a way.

» **Actions.** Philosophy also drives the "how" of ministry, which is our actions. Actions are the programs, the day-to-day implementation of the ministry philosophy that God has given you. This includes how the community is reached, how biblical community is created, and how students gather around God's Word.

While theology doesn't change, our philosophy may. That's OK. But our actions should change over time. Student ministries shouldn't be doing the same things the same way they did 10 years ago. For example, today we engage students on social media platforms, and they can even watch a service online! That was unheard of 10 years ago. Can you imagine only communicating with students by phone call? Impossible!

To create a pathway, study who God is, evaluate how you will do ministry based on those truths, and then execute programming that develops students to be more like Jesus. Prayerfully consider which programs/environments will facilitate growth and attach them to your pathway. Your pathway should be unique to the student ministry God has led you to.

WHY USE A DISCIPLESHIP PATHWAY?

A pathway is an action step to a vision statement. Have you ever noticed a church with a vision statement on a wall, bulletin, or website that never gets put into action? I've seen handouts that look phenomenal and sound great, but there are no concrete steps to actually make them come to fruition. Philosophy is great but we must take action. The pathway helps us focus on the areas that are most important to a student's growth. Since we don't naturally drift toward simplicity, it's a fight to remain focused on what really matters.

If you've been at the beach and gone in the ocean, you understand drift. As a dad, one of my roles when we go to the beach is to be the pack mule. I will do everything I can to get chairs, the cooler, toys, boogie boards, and whatever else we need in one trip from the car to beach. Regardless of how I look, I'm not going back a second time.

When everything is set up and the family is in the water, one of the ways we know where we are on the beach is by locating our massive pile of stuff. The family runs to the water, plays, splashes, and celebration ensues. Drift happens when the family is no longer in front or parallel to the pile of stuff that we established as a placeholder in the sand. In fact, due to wind and tides, it's normal to be gently pushed down the beach from your starting point. Without them noticing, the ocean moves frolickers down the beach. Then they have to get out, walk back to the pile and start over.

Without a discipleship pathway, our ministry can drift from what we say is really important. Many great ideas turn into events and opportunities and before long, a glance up reveals we aren't anywhere close to being where we wanted to be. Ministry becomes very busy, maybe even with many great things, but it isn't accomplishing what is important.

THE PATHWAY PROVIDES CLARITY

Using a discipleship pathway shows us how to program effectively. If your ministry is like most, there are probably more than enough events and programs on the calendar. What's missing is clarity on why these events and programs are there. So much time, money, and effort is spent to keep students busy, rather than focusing on intentional discipleship.

Many plans could probably be described as fellowship. There is a place for those times of fellowship, and they certainly are important, but if a majority of your programming is designed to simply gather students to hang out, then you have perfected fellowship. Unfortunately, the church has been great at fellowship, but often completely lacked in discipleship. Create space for relationships to be built while also making disciples.

The pathway brings clarity because it shows us what we need to keep doing, stop doing, and what programs need to be redeemed. Once you have created your discipleship pathway and are certain how you will make disciples, begin to evaluate each program. Using the labels keep, stop, and redeem, consider changing your programming and how you develop students. After completely analyzing how programs and events actually help make student disciples, consider one of these three options for existing programming.

KEEP
Keep is just as it sounds: It means this program or event is moving students toward a closer relationship with God. Maybe it needs some tweaking, but ultimately this is creating the environment you want your students to engage.

When I first came to Long Hollow, student Life Groups were already an important part of the programming. Leaders and students were building relationships in community, and students were growing spiritually and understanding the pathway, so it made sense to keep Life Groups. There was no need for a change because we were moving in the right direction with these groups.

One tweak that had to be made was the meeting time for groups. Groups were happening on Sunday morning at 9:30 a.m. That's a great time to host groups, as students and leaders were already on campus. The issue is that groups were only happening at 9:30 a.m. on Sunday. In effect, any student who wanted to be part of a group but couldn't come at that time was not able to participate. In reality, we were saying, "If you can't come at this time, you can't be in a group." So, we added group times outside of that time to accommodate more students.

STOP

Friday nights at our student ministry were wildly popular when I served in Miami. We had an event on Friday nights that was not part of our pathway. It was a blast. Students were coming from the community, we gave out free burgers, and offered a ton of fun. The gospel was shared briefly, but emphasis was on gathering students. In a short period of time, hundreds of students were showing up. From a numbers perspective, it was a crazy success.

Student services were on Saturday night and Sunday morning, with four options of the same service. Even with a lot of effort, we could not connect students to our regular student services or any other part of the pathway. So, Friday nights were a stand alone gathering, very similar in style to our existing student programming. After prayer and discussion, Fridays were canceled and the money, energy, and volunteers were focused on the weekend service. It was an incredibly wise decision. Our weekends improved and grew dramatically.

The pathway not only shows us what to stop doing, but also keeps us from starting things that rob us of momentum. I love it when volunteers, parents, or staff have great ideas about an event, but if it doesn't line up with how we make disciples, then it is not implemented. I'm convinced people love to suggest and participate in events because the church is putting them on. But, if the people who came up with these ideas were tasked with overseeing the events, their interest in participating probably wouldn't be as strong.

Be wise enough to discern between what actually helps students grow spiritually and what is popular because you are planning, paying for, and running it. Constantly weigh the reality of what works and what is sideways energy. Narrow the focus and embrace the courage to change what isn't helping to make disciples.

REDEEM

Camp has been a phenomenal experience at Long Hollow for many years, long before I came on staff. Many students attend, give their lives to Jesus, and are baptized. It's also an incredibly fun time. When we evaluated camp and the pathway, it was easy to see that it would be silly to stop camp. Gathering students and sharing Jesus is a huge priority!

Because camp is important, we planned ways to utilize camp to help connect students to the pathway. Strategic, intentional opportunities to take their next step are given throughout the week of camp. When students return home, we follow up with them and place them into groups of their respective choices. Redeeming camp wasn't difficult. Students were given an opportunity to learn and to take their next step on the pathway.

THE PATHWAY PROVIDES ALIGNMENT

I recently drove my truck through some rough terrain and knocked the front wheels out of alignment. It didn't seem like a big deal at first, but turned out to be costly. When the wheels are not aligned, the tires are not moving the same way, and one tire pulls a different direction. As a result, tires wear out faster and make the vehicle more difficult to drive. Similarly, when our ministry is out of alignment, it will gravitate toward distractions rather than the vision. Having a clear pathway aligns the ministry around the values that make disciples.

You've probably heard the old saying, "Show me your bank statement and I'll show you what's important to you." In student ministry, we say something similar, "Show me your friends, and I'll show you who you are becoming." Both statements are true because they reflect what we are actually doing versus what we think we're doing. There is often a large gap between who ministries say they are and what they really do. The pathway helps us align two important things in particular: our budgets and our calendars.

1. Budget. Money spent indicates what is valued. For example, most student pastors would say missions is important but budget very little for reaching others. Our budget shows the gap that exists between what we say and what we do.

Once programs have been aligned around the pathway, budget accordingly. Spend the money where God is leading you to disciple students. Regardless of the size of the budget, this is true. Your budget may depend on students to pay for everything the ministry does, so be sure you are only asking them to pay for what is helping them grow.

2. **Calendar.** Sometimes ministry can feel like a Cheesecake Factory menu. Don't get me wrong, the Thai Lettuce Wraps are unbelievable, but the menu is so packed full of options it's difficult to choose what to eat. (But seriously, try the wraps.)

Students shouldn't be overwhelmed with ministry options. When there are a plethora of events or programs to choose from, students get analysis paralysis. Much like choosing form the menu, it's confusing and easier to do nothing than to filter out options and decide.

In his book, *Tyranny of the Urgent*, Charles Hummel said, "Your greatest danger is letting the urgent things crowd out the important."[6] A pathway helps us say no to seemingly good, but ultimately unhelpful, programming. There is no lack of "good things" a student ministry can do, but the wise and focused will determine which things could have lasting impact.

THE PATHWAY SHOWS US HOW TO MEASURE

A popular conversation is the importance of numbers and measuring in student ministry. An argument could be made that counting students isn't important and that God is far more concerned with quality. Another viewpoint is that without numbers, we can't cast vision and celebrate what God has done.

There is a tension we hold in both hands when talking about numbers. On one hand, the amount of students that walk into your services doesn't necessarily equal quality ministry or spiritual growth. On the other hand, numbers represent individual souls that matter to God. Being a steward of the people God has entrusted to us also compels us to know who has been missing and why.

The bigger question is this: why measure? Don't measure numbers to impress other people; you will never be satisfied. Be diligent about your numbers to shepherd your students and finances well, then celebrate what

God is doing with your people. Knowing our numbers helps us set goals for where God is leading. Counting indicates where people are in their spiritual journey.

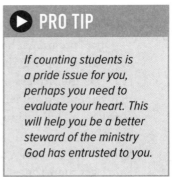

▶ **PRO TIP**

If counting students is a pride issue for you, perhaps you need to evaluate your heart. This will help you be a better steward of the ministry God has entrusted to you.

Measuring and celebration are important because what is celebrated will be cultivated in the culture. With a plan to disciple students, a narrowed focus, and clarity on what is important, you can measure differently. Here's an example of how to measure using a pathway:

HOW DO WE MEASURE SUCCESS?

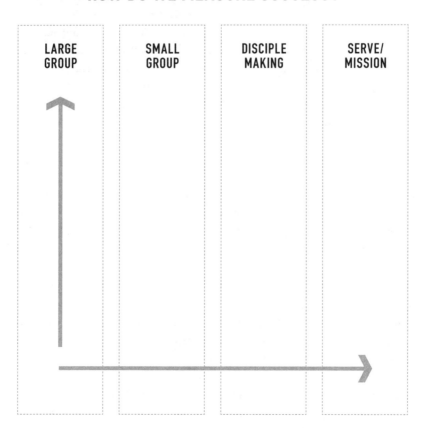

LARGE GROUP   SMALL GROUP   DISCIPLE MAKING   SERVE/ MISSION

A pathway shows us how to measure horizontally, not vertically. Instead of just measuring the large group gathering, each aspect of the pathway is included. Displaying these numbers shows how well students are moving through the pathway. By measuring each step of the pathway, there is a clear picture of movement.

For example, large group programming represents 100 percent of the students who come to your ministry. From student night, movement to sequential programs is the goal. Lets say 30 percent of students are in groups, only five percent are in discipleship, and 15 percent in serving. This type of measurement shows us where we are failing to connect students. Measuring only the large group won't ever paint the whole picture of discipleship.

Earlier in the chapter, the *Within Reach* data showed why students step out of church when they graduate from high school. I highlighted why they leave, but want to end the chapter with why they stay. What makes the difference?

WHY STUDENTS STAY

A number of factors contribute to students remaining in church after high school graduation. The top two reasons are of particular importance for student ministry programming. Understanding what keeps students after they leave must influence programming while they still attend our churches.

Surprisingly, great teaching, big name artists, and the game where students guess what leaders ate by smelling their breath aren't what made the top of the list. Although those are awesome, those moments don't have the long lasting effect we often attribute to them.

"Three or more adult influencers" is the biggest reason students stayed in church.[7] The role that adults play in the lives of students cannot be underestimated. Students leading students is great in a few capacities, but nothing replaces the voice of a mature Christ follower who disciples students.

The second greatest reason is Bible engagement. Students who can read and navigate the Bible on their own faired far better than those who can't.[8] Have you ever seen students nod along with what you were saying, yet it just didn't seem to be sinking in? Such is the case with Bible engagement in student ministry. We know it's important, but hope that it will happen at home or that students will do it because it's mentioned from the stage. Truthfully, that is a terrible strategy. We must teach and show our students how to embrace the Word. Discipleship done well encourages relationship and teaches students how to engage the Bible.

The Great Commission compels us to raise the standard for students. If we develop a strategy that doesn't include making disciples, then we have abandoned the calling God has given us.

» QUESTIONS

1. How could having a clearly defined discipleship pathway affect your ministry?

2. What is the theology and philosophy of your current programming? What might need to change?

3. What are some obstacles you face when creating a pathway? Identify one step you could take this week to begin overcoming each obstacle.

4. List the top ten attributes you would love to see true of students who are graduating from your ministry. How does your ministry prepare them to leave?

5. What is one thing you need to keep? Stop? Redeem?

7 MAKING DISCIPLES WHO MAKE DISCIPLES

"One must decide where he wants his ministry to count—in the momentary applause of the popular recognition or in the reproduction of his life in a few chosen men who will carry on his work after he is gone."[1]

ROBERT COLEMAN

DAVID KING WAS THE LAUNCH COMMANDER AT NASA for more than 30 years. He was responsible for over 125 launches in his tenure, including the Space Shuttles Challenger and Columbia. He's a brilliant man, but more importantly, he loves Jesus and is committed to serving Him.

When he talks about NASA, the wisdom and experience he brings to the table make the missions come to life. The strategy, intentionality, and dedication to these missions are awe inspiring. Millions of small details—like having launch pads near the equator so the shuttle can get an extra 900 miles per hour—go into each mission.

I enjoy watching shuttle launches, and it seems I'm not alone. Historically, massive crowds have shown up to launch sites in great anticipation. From the TV angles, you would never know that the closest you can get to the launch pad is three miles away; any closer and you risk having a heart attack from the vibration. The launch isn't the first phase of the operation, but is vitally important if the mission is to continue, whether it's to the Space Station, the moon, or to defeat Megatron. The mission starts with training and practice years before the countdown ever begins. No one sees these parts. People see launches though, anticipating how humanity will go beyond what we know, attempting to do what's never been done before.

With far greater implications than traveling through space, Christians have been given the mission to make disciples—and student ministry is a launchpad for students to live out the command. But sometimes we get sidetracked from our mission and don't follow through. Part of the reason we lose focus is that we are better at connecting students to the ministry or our events than we are at connecting them to the Word of God. This detour isn't intentional, though. Mission drift happens when there is no clear strategy in place.

We lose our focus on the most important thing by focusing on too many things. Emphasis on getting students to attend our service and keep showing up can be overwhelming. Excellent programming, follow up, church activities, and meeting the needs of many people can occupy so much time that the mission to make disciples gets lost in the clutter. If students leave our services impressed by what we did, but not inspired to know more of Jesus, we have failed.

It's not wrong to make student ministry awesome or to challenge your students to come and hang out. That is an absolute necessity in student ministry. But if all of these efforts keep us from completing the mission Christ has called us to, then we are short of finishing the task.

Think back to the time when Jesus left the disciples with the command to make other disciples. What if the disciples just encouraged people to come to church? What if the early church wasn't concerned with making disciples and only focused on what happened inside the church? It could be argued with great fervor that the church would look very different today.

Our programming is leading us somewhere, and it should be toward completing the mission Christ gave us. If your answer is, "We will do what they did 20 years ago!" I'd politely ask you to pause, view the current state of the western church, and then reconsider. We are wise when we invest in the only two things that are eternal: people and God's Word. Those two things are not mutually exclusive, the Word changes people forever.

Discipleship is described many ways. Some would say, "I'm discipling my students—we hang out, play video games, and talk." Others would sum up discipleship by saying, "We talk about life's challenges, and I help them."

? GUT CHECK QUESTION

If everyone discipled their students like you, what would the church be like in 20 years?

Relational moments are good and necessary, but remember that discipleship is specifically focused on spiritual growth. Discipleship is intentionally entering into someone's life to help them know and follow Jesus and obey His teachings. The apostle Paul stated the mission this way:

What you have heard from me in the presence
of many witnesses, commit to faithful men
who will be able to teach others also.
2 TIMOTHY 2:2

He also made this appeal to the Christians at Phillipi.

Do what you have learned and received and heard from me,
and seen in me, and the God of peace will be with you.
PHILIPPIANS 4:9

Paul was prescribing for us what Jesus did with the disciples. Jesus is the ultimate disciple maker and our example. He invested heavily in the 12 disciples and eventually released them to do ministry. Notice the progression of how He trained the disciples. First, Jesus ministered to others while the disciples watched Him heal the sick and forgive sins. After some time, Jesus allowed the disciples to assist as He ministered, like when he fed the 5,000 (Matt. 14:13-21). In Mark 9, Jesus assisted the disciples as they ministered when a father brought Him his demon possessed son. Lastly, we see Jesus command them to go and minister, promising that He would be with them (Acts 1:8).

This is a natural progression of a deepening relationship and growth that leads the disciples to greater maturity. Jesus prepared them for years before He launched them into ministry on their own. A glance at the Book of Mark shows us how Jesus spent time with His disciples. He went to their homes, ate with them, met their families, went boating with them, and withdrew from everyone else to teach them. Discipleship isn't just about sermons and Bible studies—it's about doing life together.

Discipleship is more than a transfer of information, it's transformation. Jesus didn't approach His disciples with a paperback book, He spent His life with them. Transformation happens when a leader teaches and models Jesus, and the student begins to imitate Christ.

It is pretty obvious that discipleship is not a quick fix, drive-through operation. It takes time to invest in and develop others, which is frustrating to many church leaders. In churches where an unhealthy culture of rapid growth, comparisons to others, and a "just try harder" mantra exist, the beauty of discipleship has been lost in the wake of these competitive philosophies. I've spoken to many church leaders who love the idea of discipleship and believe it should be part of the church, but they grow frustrated and abandon it because it isn't measurable. When I shared a vision for discipleship in student ministry, a pastor once told me (no exaggeration), "OK, but you can't measure that. Don't waste time on that." My heart sank. How did the desire for more people in the church cancel out the mission God gave us? Why can't evangelism and discipleship coexist?

Discipleship and evangelism are two sides of the same Great Commission coin. Francis Chan gave a great example of how many churches respond to discipleship. He said that if he told his daughter to clean her room, it would be odd if she simply told him she'd memorized what he told her to do, learned to say his command in Greek, or gathered with her friends to talk about cleaning her room.[2] All he wanted her to do was clean her room! The church often repeats the mission, studies the mission, and learns to communicate it creatively. All of those things have their place but not at the expense of completing the mission. God wants us to obey Him. The church's need to impress others and prioritize other things has suppressed discipleship. If Jesus modeled discipleship for us and told us to do it, then to ignore what He said is nothing short of disobedience.

Discipleship changed my life. There have been a few men over the years who have discipled me, and I am different as a result. Because I have been discipled, I see the value and want others to be discipled as well. If you have never been intentionally discipled, I challenge you to find someone of the same gender and more mature in the faith to invest in you.

IMPLEMENT DISCIPLESHIP IN YOUR MINISTRY

Like being discipled, creating a discipleship culture takes time. Consider implementing discipleship ministry-wide as a next step for those in your student ministry. (See Chapter 6.) Consider launching discipleship groups— also called d-groups—as a weekly part of your programming. The groups usually consist of three to five students, are led by an adult, are gender specific, and meet weekly during specific times of the year. Use the school year as a guide for when groups meet and take a break. If school is in session, groups are meeting. Summer time can be difficult with vacations and inconsistency of the students' schedules but may work well in your context.

Why only three to five students? Learning and accountability works well in smaller groups. There isn't pressure on just one person and the members can learn from each other. There's also positive peer pressure to show up and do the work. Plus, the group dynamic creates a great environment for dialogue, and encourages students to see their friends grow in their faith.

When launching, start with a small focus. Depending on the size of your ministry, start with just a few d-groups in the beginning. If it's just one group—that's OK. Hand pick the students you want to disciple and plan to meet for the next year. As the students in your group grow, they will share the excitement with others. If launching a more than one group, choose some leaders you can disciple who will then lead groups. This way, everyone who is leading a group has experienced being in a discipleship group.

When first coming to Long Hollow, my pastor wanted to see discipleship implemented for everyone. First, he discipled the staff. It was a larger than normal d-group—just over 25 of us—but each week, he would walk us through a d-group time. After meeting, we would all go to lunch together. (Yes, there were 25 people at lunch. It was awesome!) I definitely don't recommend a d-group of 25, but for a short season with staff, it made sense. And because the staff had experienced what a d-group is like, we could lead groups in a healthy way.

HOW D-GROUPS WORK

D-groups usually meet for 1 to 1.5 hours and at a time that works for the schedules of everyone in the group. If you go to a Cracker Barrel, Panera Bread, or Chick-fil-A on a Tuesday or Wednesday morning in the Hendersonville, Tennessee area, you will see student groups. You can also find them on a church campus, at Starbucks, or in people's homes. To encourage engagement, we permit freedom of where and when to meet.

Once these groups begin, they are closed to new participants. The strategy behind closing the group is simple: students are unlikely to open up and be transparent about their struggles if new people keep showing up. D-groups are based on honesty and trust, so keeping the group closed creates space for that.

D-groups usually meet for one to two years after forming. If you follow the school schedule, consider holidays and vacation time, it's actually only

14-16 months or so of meeting. One year of meeting is only about seven to eight months time and is considerably short in the grand scheme of things.

After meeting for two years, groups should replicate. Why? Because d-groups are a launchpad, not a landing site. Replication happens when students who have been discipled stop meeting in their group to launch new ones. For example, after two years of meeting at a designated time a group of three students should dissolve. Then, each member should find two or three new friends and launch a new discipleship group. What began as three students in a group is now three groups with nine students. This is how discipleship continues to grow.

WHAT D-GROUP TIME LOOKS LIKE

Discipleship groups incorporates several spiritual disciplines. Like the example given in Chapter 6, it's like steadily raising the rope higher and higher. Practicing the disciplines each week will help students develop a love for biblical community and the Word of God. Each week, the group will memorize a Scripture verse, do five days of Bible reading, and journal about what they have learned. Accountability can thrive in these groups when the Word is being read and transparent conversations take place.

STEP 1: CATCHING UP

Group time starts with conversation and catching up. This allows everyone to hear what's been going on in each others' lives and reduces talking between the students later on. As students share, listen closely for things to celebrate, what to pray about, and which areas need accountability. Sometimes asking specific questions helps get the conversation started. Ask them something they are thankful for, something they are celebrating, or a struggle they may have. This conversation could last the whole 90 minutes, so you'll have to moderate well.

STEP 2: ACCOUNTABILITY

Accountability questions help students process areas of struggle. Whatever questions you ask, the goal isn't condemnation but restoration. If students have fallen, encourage them to repent and build them back up. Provide ways to overcome temptation and do your best to keep in touch more than once a week to lift them up. Here are a few good examples of accountability questions:

>> Did you view anything immoral this week?
>> Were you honest with your parents?
>> Did you honor God with your physical behavior this week?

STEP 3: SCRIPTURE MEMORY VERSES

Ideally, Scripture verse memorization is next, and the group recites the verse they have agreed to memorize. Those who just started memorizing on the way into the meeting may have some difficulty remembering. Those who worked on memorizing the verse throughout the week are usually able to recite it with ease. Memorize whatever verses the Lord leads you to, but also consider memorizing whole chapters or passages. If the group memorizes a verse a week, then over the course of the time the d-group meets together they will potentially memorize a whole chapter or more. How great would it be for students to memorize a whole passage of Scripture that applies to everyday life?

STEP 4: STUDY THE WORD

Studying the Word together is the heart of the gathering time. Hopefully, the group will choose a Bible reading plan for the year. Five days a week for a reading plan is a great approach. Leaving two days of the week open allows for catch up if any of the days are missed.

 PRO TIP

If you don't have a reading plan, I highly recommend choosing one from Replicate, a disciple making organization. You can get more information on a H.E.A.R journal at replicate.org/foundations.

The expectation is that the group will engage with the Word for five days each week and journal about what they are learning. There are several ways to journal, so whichever works best for your students is the one you should use. We love using the H.E.A.R. Journal. H.E.A.R. stands for highlight, explain, apply, and respond.

Students sharing from their journals opens the door to conversations about what they are learning from God's Word. The key of d-groups is for students to fall in love with God and His Word and then grow from what they have learned. When the group is reading the same passages and learning from them, there is great traction for conversation.

STEP 5: PRAYER

Close the group with prayer time. You've listened to what they are happy about, what they struggle with and what God is teaching them, so have them pray for each other based on the conversations you have just had.

THE MARCS OF A DISCIPLE

Spiritual growth is difficult to measure by numeric value, but don't let that discourage you. Scripture gives us some clear passages that reveal what spiritual growth looks like. Check out these verses in Psalm 119.

*How can a young man keep his way
pure? By keeping your word.
I have sought you with all my heart; don't let me
wander from your commands. I have treasured your
word in my heart so that I may not sin against you. LORD,
may you be blessed; teach me your statutes.
With my lips I proclaim all the judgments from your mouth.
I rejoice in the way revealed by your
decrees as much as in all riches.
I will meditate on your precepts and think about your ways.
I will delight in your statutes; I will not forget your word.*
PSALM 119:9-16

Although these verses don't say, "This is the product of discipleship," they do reveal someone who has a heart for God and wants to walk with Him. We could probably agree that this person appears to be growing spiritually. We can measure spiritual growth by looking at the MARCS of a disciple. MARCS is an acronym developed by Robby Gallaty to help identify if someone is growing in their faith. Each letter is representative of a marker of spiritual growth in a believers life.

M IS FOR MISSIONAL.

Someone who lives missionally knows and understands the Great Commission. Whether at home, school, or on a trip somewhere, this person consistently lives out and shares their faith. D-groups are a vital part of encouraging students to live out their faith. Have the group to share the names of their lost friends and pray for their salvation. Each person should pray for an opportunity in the coming week to share Jesus with the person being prayed for. Celebrate when the student has the courage to share Jesus.

A youth pastor friend named Jason shares the story of Gerald, a guy in his student ministry. Gerald shared his faith consistently at his school, but over the last year, not one person had responded positively to the gospel. His mom noticed and was concerned that Gerald would be discouraged if someone didn't give their life to Jesus. Mom approached the youth pastor as they were boarding a plane to Jamaica on a mission trip. She asked Jason to pray for Gerald as he shared and to pray specifically someone would give their life to Christ. Jason agreed and they left for the Caribbean.

Two days into the trip, Gerald led a man to Christ. Jason was elated! He told Gerald, "Your mom and I have been praying someone would get saved so you wouldn't get discouraged!" Gerald, unshaken, looked at Jason and said, "I'm not sharing the gospel just so people get saved. I'm sharing it to be obedient." Lesson learned.

What a powerful truth. We're not the ones who do the saving—God does. We are simply commanded to go and share the Good News. So, it's time to celebrate when someone shares the gospel, regardless of how people respond. Continue to impress on students the importance of living out their faith and how the gospel changes us every day.

D-groups can very easily become inward focused, though. If we're not lovingly nudged to think of those outside the church walls, it is easy to be consumed with ourselves. True disciples aren't consumed with self—they're consumed with Jesus. If you want to know whether or not a student is living missonally, ask yourself if the person being discipled shares their faith and/or has a desire to do so. If the answer to these questions is yes, then it's a great indicator that God is at work in their life.

A IS FOR ACCOUNTABILITY.

No doubt the most difficult but necessary part of discipleship is accountability. The notion of being transparent about struggles and sin doesn't usually happen naturally. It's tough to admit when we have sinned; it's even more difficult to acknowledge that we keep on making the same mistakes.

Accountability isn't the judge and jury, it's a shepherd that keeps sheep from wandering too far. Open conversations about temptations and shortcomings show that a person trusts that they are known, loved, and accepted in spite of their worst choices. Just like Jesus, accountability says, "I love you the way that you are, but I refuse to leave you that way." Grace, encouragement, and the safety of being able to share without fear of gossip encourages speaking the truth because accountability isn't broadcasting another persons shortcomings.

I discipled one particular group of guys for a few years. They were new believers when we started, and accountability was very direct. Some struggled with having sex with their girlfriends, another with drugs, and one with stealing. The approach for discipling them was different than discipling a group of seasoned Christians. One means of accountability that the guys asked for was my checking text messages on their phones. Most of them were sexting girls, and they wanted to see that part of their lives redeemed. We agreed that at any random time, I could ask for their phones to be passed to me and they would do it. This was their idea! One night, only part way through the study, I stopped and asked them to pass their phones. Each guy reached in his pocket and started passing them over, except one, who was hunched over and clutching his phone. I realized immediately he was deleting his text messages! The other guys in the group began to heckle him. I didn't have to say anything—the peer pressure from the other guys in the group said it all. Each of those guys today will tell you that knowing they were going to be accountable for how they texted helped them change their ways. Of course the Holy Spirit was the primary motivator, but having someone who would check up on and encourage them helped the process.

Your methods probably look different, but the accountability aspect is the same. Show love to students by walking through their struggles with them. Welcoming accountability isn't easy, but a desire to move away from the old ways into the new life shows a desire for growth.

R IS FOR REPLICATING

Several times in the Book of Acts, we learn about the church growing. In Acts 2, three thousand people were added to the Church in one day (v. 41)! Later in that same chapter, Scripture says the Lord added daily those who were being saved (v. 47). What we see in the early church is not an example of addition, but rather a multiplication of new believers. The church grew because believers were living out their faith, sharing everything they had, and were committed to God's Word (vv. 42-47). As the people grew in their faith, the church grew too.

The purpose of discipleship is for students to grow in their faith. As a result, the church should be impacted by those who are following Jesus passionately. When groups replicate, the church grows and is influenced by these growing Christians. When students want their friends to know Jesus and be discipled, they are becoming disciple makers. They are passionate about what God is passionate about and developing a heart for others.

C IS FOR COMMUNAL

Jean is the CEO of a growing company and leads a girls discipleship group for high school seniors. She has her own kids, grandkids, and a house to take care of, yet is one of the best examples of a d-group leader I've ever seen. She meets with her girls weekly and communicates well with them when they aren't meeting. The girls come to her house to eat and have fun together. Jean goes to their ball games and recitals, but most importantly, she engages them in discipleship each week.

Not everyone can be like Jean and shouldn't try to be. But her example can still teach much about discipleship. Discipleship is more than just a weekly meeting—it's life together. The "master teacher" role in d-groups doesn't work too well for fostering relationships. It's far easier to dominate conversation, give answers without asking questions, and treat the group members like attendees than it is to invest time. We see the opposite example in Jesus. Desiring biblical community and encouragement to keep growing are great indicators that life change is happening.

S IS FOR SCRIPTURAL

The Bible is central to discipleship. If students fall in love with the Word, their lives will change. God speaks to us, convicts us, and guides us as we digest the truth. Books about God and the Christian life are helpful, but they are no substitute for God's Word. Be careful not to replace the Bible with a popular guys or girls book. Leaders can be guilty of gravitating to books that have influenced them, rather than focusing on Scripture.

Use other books after you have consumed the Word together. Read those as a supplement to what God is teaching you. Take a look at what Paul teaches the Thessalonians about the power of engaging God's Word.

This is why we constantly thank God, because when you received the word of God that you heard from us, you welcomed it not as a human message, but as it truly is, the word of God, which also works effectively in you who believe.
1 THESSALONIANS 2:13

A passion for God's Word is an obvious sign that a student is growing in their faith. Encourage them to continue by engaging the Word with them.

Discipling students is a launch pad that will send them on a mission for the rest of their life. When discipled well, students will love God and His Word and want others to know Him. The mission doesn't start when they step out of high school, it starts long before on the early mornings at Chick-Fil-A with an open Bible.[3]

>> QUESTIONS

1. What does discipleship look like in your ministry?

2. Would you be satisfied in 20 years if the church disciples like you do now? Why or why not?

3. Do you currently have accountability in your own life? What does it look like?

4. What are three characteristics of spiritually growing students in your ministry?

8 > ATTRACTING STUDENTS TO YOUR MINISTRY

> "You can make excuses or you can make progress, but you can't make both."[1]
>
> **CRAIG GROESCHEL**

TYLER WAS A YOUNG STUDENT PASTOR in a suburb of Nashville. God placed him at a church and in a neighborhood where 90 percent of the people around him didn't look like him. Because this area is in the South, cultural differences could have been a factor. Some church folks scratched their heads, others (not so) quietly guessed how long this would last.

Tyler plunged into life with his new church family. There wasn't a big budget or many resources, but he loved and shepherded them well. It wasn't long before ridiculous amounts of students began showing up at this quiet little church's student ministry every Wednesday night.

Student pastors at camps and other events would look at the group and say out loud, "There's no way that's the student guy at that church." Some would say the odds were stacked against Tyler—low funding, different cultures, and a small church. But none of that seemed to be a factor in reaching students in the surrounding neighborhoods.

We are generally better at making excuses for why students don't come to our churches than we are at creating opportunities to engage with them. It's easy to have a "woe is me" attitude when things aren't going your way. The big question is: What will you do about it?

We've established that bragging about your attendance is unproductive, but that doesn't change our commitment to see the local church grow. You can love Jesus and want to see more people love Him too. So, let's talk about how to attract students to your ministry. But first, let's agree that there's no formula that works the same everywhere. There is no singular sure-fire method that will always work. And it's rarely just one idea that attracts students—it's a combination of several.

TEACH THE BIBLE

Don't sleep on this point. If you have been in ministry for a while, you may read this and think: "I know what he's going to say." If you're tempted to move to the next item, don't. Hang with me here. This is vital to your ministry and the students you serve.

The western church is at a crossroads. Some churches are choosing to use less of Scripture in an attempt to make lost people feel comfortable. We must consider—if the Word is barely used, presented out of context, or omitted entirely from our teaching time—what separates our teaching from a great pep talk? Are we able to communicate better than Jesus, Paul, and many others who used Scripture to teach? There is no manufactured conviction or emotionally charged guilt trip that can replace what God says to us.

For the word of God is living and effective and sharper than any double-edged sword, penetrating as far as the separation of soul and spirit, joints and marrow. It is able to judge the thoughts and intentions of the heart.
HEBREWS 4:12

God's Word brings conviction and clarity like nothing else can.

For I am not ashamed of the gospel, because it is the power of God for salvation to everyone who believes, first to the Jew, and also to the Greek. For in it the righteousness of God is revealed from faith to faith, just as it is written: The righteous will live by faith.
ROMANS 1:16-17

Will some walk away because the truth of Scripture is too difficult for them? Yes, and to be truthful, that's hard to watch. Hopefully as you build strong relationships with the students in your ministry, they will learn to trust that you speak the truth to them out of love. In His Word, God clearly states the truth for the same reason. Model His love for them by sharing the truth no matter what.

Our teaching is calling students to follow something. If what we have impressed on students doesn't include God's Word, what are we calling them to? How do we call them to follow Jesus if we don't trust His Word enough to teach it? We can't perpetuate Bible illiteracy:

» **The Bible is as relevant today as it was 2000 years ago.** Don't go to great lengths to prove that it matters today, simply allow students to see how influential it is in your life and they will be convinced.

» **The Word changes lives.** It sends a powerful message when students are being saved and their lives are being transformed into the image of Christ. Other students want to be a part of that change.

» **Teaching the Bible brings conviction for sin and shows the need for a Savior.** In partnership with the Holy Spirit, teaching the Word also grows students into mature believers who care for lost people.

» **New life in Christ will always attract new life.** We teach the Bible out of faithfulness to God, and students showing up to engage and hear more are byproducts of that.

» **Students who are affected by the Word also see the need for others to know God.** It's reciprocal in nature, just like we saw in Acts 2.

» **Most of all, study and prepare well, but let the Holy Spirit through His Word do the work**.

BE WHERE THE STUDENTS ARE

Take a moment and list the top six places students from your community spend their time. While each community is different, we find that most students hang out in similar places.

This is not a trick question. If your students spend most of their time in the places you listed, how often are you present there with them? Your presence matters. Student ministry can be summed up in one word: *relationships*. The heart of everything we do is centered around a relationship with God and a relationship with students.

▶ PRO TIP

Be careful! Don't show up places so students will come to your event. They will see right through that.

Everyone on earth wants to be known and loved, this isn't unique to students. Being present with them where they are shows that they are valuable, heard, and seen. If the only time they see us is when we invite them to come to our thing, the message we send is that they are only valuable when they show up. Doing life where they live shows that the care and concern you talk about having for them on stage is reality.

A high school pastor friend of mine, Morris, explained how a conversation with a student changed the way he approached going to where students are. He went to hang out often, particularly on Wednesday, to make sure all the students knew to come to Wednesday night service. It was also common for Morris to show up with fliers for camp and other events. He stopped to invite a guy to a tournament the student ministry was having and the student said to him, "You only come here and talk to me when you want me to come to your event." The student was right. Morris was crushed. His motives were exposed, and he hadn't even realized it.

When you spend time where students are, do it because you love them and want to spend time with them. Don't look at them as an opportunity to advance what you are doing. Will students come as a result? Of course, but your motivation matters. Armed with the right perspective, engage students where they live.

SCHOOLS

I'm still amazed how often student ministry leaders don't engage schools. Most students in your area are in the schools. I realize it can be intimidating for some and others may think they are too busy. I've even heard some senior pastors don't want the student person out of the office enough to go to the school. But sitting in your office all day isn't helping you do what God has called you to do. Get out among the people, build relationships, and have some fun.

Every school district is different in what they will allow. So, only do what you are allowed. If you break the rules, you will cause more restrictions and hurt everyone else.

During my first two years in Miami, schools were very difficult to engage. The school board was cautious about allowing any churches in because of past student pastors' behavior. So, we just began to serve the schools with no agenda. Painting, mulching, pressure washing—we served however we could. Eventually, they began to trust that we were *for* the school, not ourselves, and they let us engage. A beautiful partnership with over 40 schools in Miami-Dade county resulted.

Don't use restrictions as an excuse. Figure out what you can do and work from there. Sports teams are usually the most popular way to serve. There are opportunities to be a assistant coaches or chaplains, bring snacks, buy team dinners, and so on. Attend the games, go to practices, and support their causes by being visible and volunteering. Most student ministries engage with sports teams because it's relatively easy to do so. Even if you aren't a sports fan, don't let that hinder you from engaging. Students care far more about how you treat them than if you were a star quarterback.

Of course we should minister to athletes, but those teams represent a small portion of the school's student body. A popular thought is, "If you win a popular jock, they will reach everyone else in their school." That was true years ago, but not as much anymore. Don't hang your influence on one particular group or person.

The band, orchestra, and choir are great places to spend time with students as well. These creative and talented people are often overlooked by ministries because they aren't deemed as influential. We have seen great fruit come from spending time with these clubs. I've seen several student pastors hang around a baseball team and completely neglect the teenagers in the area of the arts. Engage students wherever you can!

Support the school's drama team, Future Farmers of America, 4-H Club, or whatever club could use your support. Go check out the drama team's next play or attend the choir performance—it may not be your thing, but students will be elated to see you there. Every student matters to God, so let's find ways to reach them.

Volunteer at the school whenever possible. Drop by and visit the principal just to encourage them. Let them know that your church and student ministry love and support them. Show up from time to time with donuts or bagels for the teachers.

Enlist the students to minister to the teachers. A few years ago, we

> ▶ **PRO TIP**
>
> *Treat the front office staff well. They are the gatekeepers to much of the school. If they know you and trust you, your time on campus can be much more profitable.*

started gathering students on a teacher workday to show love to the teachers. Breakfast was provided by the church, and the students helped make pancakes and serve the teachers. Sometimes, while the teachers were being served breakfast, the students brought equipment to wash their cars. The principal was asked the day before, and when he agreed he let the teachers know to park in a specific place to have their car washed. It was amazing.

Serving teachers is a wise investment. When teachers know that a local church loves them and supports them, trust is built. When there is difficulty or a student is struggling, that church already has a great reputation for caring for others and is often asked to help. When you serve, you win in multiple areas.

HOMESCHOOL KIDS

In many places, the homeschool movement is growing. Understandably, safety concerns and dangers of some school systems have parents undertaking the daunting task of educating their children themselves.

Shephathiah is a middle school pastor. His team is very engaged in both public and private schools every day of the week. Last school year, he noticed that homeschool kids were not being engaged like other students in the ministry. He decided that homeschool students would be invited to come to the church for two hours every Thursday. They hang out, eat some snacks, have fun, and study the Bible together. In this case, there was no central place where homeschool students hung out, so he created one. It's different than showing up at a school, but works in this scenario. We must consistently find new ways to engage students outside of church services and programming.

Where are the other places your students spend their time? The lake or the beach? Recreation leagues or the park? Clearly, some places are easier (and more fun!) to engage, but the key is to build relationships where they live. Take a moment and write down the first three places you will engage students and put a date beside each one. The date represents the deadline for you to be present with students at those places. Holding yourself accountable is difficult at first, but you will be glad you did.

1. _____   DATE: _____

2. _____   DATE: _____

3. _____   DATE: _____

CREATE ENGAGING OPPORTUNITIES

The importance of relational capital in the community cannot be overstated. However, having a place that students love to be is helpful when growing a ministry. The Bible must be central to everything we do, but making services and events fun and memorable isn't contradictory to challenging students with the truth of God's Word. There are two myths that must be debunked in order to create engaging opportunities:

1. **"My church doesn't have all the stuff that other churches have, so we can't pull it off."** I hear this sort of excuse way too often. Many churches with less resources often create engaging opportunities with what they do have. The truth is that larger churches with bigger budgets can become inflated, complacent, and rely on what they have always done. You might be surprised to know how many student pastors wish their teams had the "hunger" to go all out and try new things. Stop believing that bigger budgets are equal to better dreams, it's just not true.

2. **"That's just an attractional event."** The word *attractional* often has a negative connotation, implying that a ministry is more focused on hype and crowds than on growing students. Some ministries may get caught up in hype and crowds, but the term is regularly used to speak negatively of another ministry. Using the term *attractional* as a put down reveals a sense of "ministry envy" coming from our own hearts.

Let's pursue ministries that engage all of the areas we've talked about. Consider what an attractional, discipling, and missional ministry looks like. It makes sense to seek to attract students when you have a plan to disciple them and teach them to engage the world in a way that aligns with the ministry of Jesus. Don't draw in students to simply make a crowd—move them forward in their faith with intentionality.

⚠ A WORD OF CAUTION

Gathering students with no intent other than a fun event places the emphasis on gatherings rather than Scripture. This is when attractional events live up to the stereotype.

AFTER SERVICE EVENTS (TAG ONS)

About five years into my student ministry tenure, I learned the importance of stacking or tagging on key events to our students services. For years, my habit was to have events on a weekend night instead of when student ministry was meeting, so that's what I did. Then I realized I was missing out.

Let's say Wednesday night is when your student ministry meets during the week. Plan events and attractional times around your service. If one of the reasons for doing an event is to help students connect to your ministry, then this makes far more sense than an "off" time. Don't think that because it's a week night you can't do some incredibly cool stuff. Swamp Wars (teams and obstacle courses), Nerf Wars, basketball tournaments, dodge ball tournaments, and so on, can all be planned around a service so students can hear about and respond to Jesus. Here are a few benefits from offering tag ons.

1. **Students who come for fun the first time are actually attending a service.** They don't have to come back another night to experience what your ministry is all about.
2. **Volunteer leaders are already there, so they won't need to give up another night of their week.**
3. **You are not out another night of the week, and more importantly, the chances of students attaching to the ministry are greater.**
4. **When coordinated well, students can hear a clear gospel presentation at the service and enjoy time with their friends.**

Tag ons are a great way for students to have a blast while inviting their friends to attend a service. By the way, that's insider language. Don't advertise you're having a tag on, come up with a creative name for what you are doing. Maximize your service times by aligning opportunities for new students to come.

CAMP

God uses camp to change so many people's lives, including mine. Even as a pastor/leader at camp, I'm challenged every year and can't wait to go back. Camp is a great place for new students to connect to your ministry. I've heard it said that in terms of relational equity, one week of camp is like six months of student services. The time spent together creates special bonds. So many great things can be done in one week of camp.

A couple of years ago, a group of football players who were new to our ministry went to camp. They had attended church some when they were kids, but weren't consistently in church at this time. At first, they were intimidating to other campers. They were loud and sarcastic but actually pretty fun. During that week, the Lord began to work in their hearts.

Just a few nights in, three of them committed their lives to following Jesus. They turned in some "paraphernalia" they weren't supposed to have and began talking about what God was doing in their hearts. I was completely blown away to see one of them kneeling at his chair in the back of the room during worship the next night. Camp always reminds me that God wants to change lives.

However, we must pay careful attention to new students after camp is over. One student ministry shared that almost 40 percent of the students they took to camp didn't show up to student ministry again. That doesn't mean we shouldn't do camp, but it does mean we must be way more intentional about connecting students to ministry once we get back home. Announcing from stage, "Hey, we hope to see you all this Wednesday night after we get back" is not sufficient follow-up.

Here are four steps to engaging new students after camp:

1. **Entrust a camp leader who the student knows to follow up and invite that student to services upon return.**
2. **Encourage small group leaders to invite new students to join their small group after coming home from camp.**
3. **Encourage the core students of the ministry to build relationships with new students who they can invite and guide to be part of the ministry.**
4. **Offer a "next step" option before leaving camp.** Ask students what phase of your pathway they are on and where they would like to be. Follow up based on their responses, inviting them to walk deeper with the Lord.

A THRIVING VOLUNTEER CULTURE

Most conversations about growing student ministry don't begin with talking about volunteers. Usually, the idea is "Let's get more students, then get volunteer leaders to help." A shift in thinking must occur when considering the role of volunteer leaders. Leaders aren't the police who stand in the back and make sure the students don't make out, they are Jesus with skin on for many students.

One thought that has captured my thinking in this area is this: "Are we prepared for the students God wants to send us?" Our desire is to see more students come, but have we adequately prepared? What if God sent 20, 50, or 100 new students to your ministry in the next two months? How would you care for them well? Having capable, friendly adult leaders in place shows students that you are ready for them to show up. When trained to greet, care for, and instruct students, leaders make a profound impact on many students who have little or no godly adult influences.

How you view the role of volunteer leaders will determine how they lead. If you limit their ability, they will only go as far as you will allow. As you train and cast the vision for how they can lead, leaders will respond to opportunities within the student ministry.

Vivian is a rock star volunteer. She began serving as a table leader during the students services, lovingly guiding high school girls through the tumultuous moments of their lives. Leading a small group seemed like a natural next step, and she did so with grace. When a leadership opportunity opened to help develop student leaders, she seized the chance. She led and coached other leaders as a way to minister to them.

Leaders will grow into the opportunities you give them. Recruit them, train them, and unleash them as a force in the student ministry. Many students do not have godly parents or guardians. Well prepared volunteers not only show students the love of God, but they also model what a Christian adult is like.

AN INVITING CULTURE

Amazon is my preferred shopping destination for many reasons. Obviously, the convenience is primary. But beyond that is not having to go a physical store. When visiting a store, I usually know pretty quickly if I want to return. Is the store organized or dirty? Are the bathrooms clean? Are workers friendly?

Have you ever visited a store and the employees act like you are interrupting their social life? Few things make me want to come back to a place where I was treated like an inconvenience. People are willing to pay more for a product if the company has good customer service. Plus, after having a positive experience, they will often spend up to 140 percent more than customers who do not.[2] How a person is treated results in where they spend their time and money.

Imagine being a student who walks into church—as a guest or for the first time in a long time—and not feeling welcomed. No one wants to experience that. Create a culture that welcomes guests without embarrassing them. Make them feel recognized and known regardless of past attendance. When a student is accepted and feels like they belong, they want to keep being part of it. When student ministry is a place where students feel welcomed, their friends will also want them to come.

GIRLS MINISTRY

Girls Minister, Kate Michaelson, contributes some great thoughts on how ministering specifically to the teen girls in your church helps them feel like they belong:

"There is something special about getting all girls in a room and a female leader speaking into them. Without guys in the room, so much drama and distraction can be removed, which lends itself to a more freeing environment. The more environments where girls feel safe and valued, the more our ministries will grow. When Godly community begins to form within the girls in your ministry, the more girls will want to invite their friends into that type of sisterhood or 'girl gang.' We need women who invest in girls. Older women in your church have so much to offer your girls ministry. It's a beautiful thing when adult women lead high school girls, who, in return, lead middle school girls. This develops a culture of girls being equipped and empowered to lead. One of the best things you can do for the girls in your ministry is to create a team of women who are thinking, praying for, and planning specifically for the girls. When writing sermons or creating events and hangouts for students, it's important to think through the different audiences that are in the room. Not every girl will connect with a sports analogy. Show the girls in your ministry that they have a seat at the table, that they have a voice and can lead. Teach them that they have unique giftedness, and they can be used by God."

Regardless of your education, location or the size of your church, commit to seeing new students engage in your ministry. Evaluate what is being done and what needs to be done to effect change.

» QUESTIONS

1. What has been the most effective means of attracting students to your ministry?

....

....

....

....

2. What percentage of time per week do you spend with students outside of church?

....

....

....

....

3. Which of the listed ways of attracting students makes sense to you? Which ones seem odd?

....

....

....

....

4. How is the "invite culture" of your ministry? What might make it better?

....

....

....

....

DOING THINGS YOU DON'T LIKE

9

"Do or do not, there is no try."[1]

YODA

I HAVE A SERIOUS DISDAIN FOR SKUNKS. There is an argument that if the rodent-type offender has their spray glands taken out, the striped bandit will make a great pet. As entertaining as that sounds, it's a hard pass from me. Outside of the non-glorious stench they produce, skunks can be pretty vicious.

I live on a farm and recently took a direct spray from a good sized skunk. It was far more horrifying than I ever imagined. The pungent odor was so strong that upon entering the house to shower, two of my boys started to vomit. It took a couple of days to get the smell out of the house, and we held a moment of silence for the University of Miami sweatshirt that had to be destroyed.

Imagine my surprise a couple of weeks later when I went to collect chicken eggs (we have around 50 chickens) and found the skunk in the nesting box! He was actually trying to sleep in the coop while pushing the chickens to survive outside in the night. He gorged himself on eggs and settled in to sleep.

I faced a predicament. I needed to remove the skunk but had zero interest in getting sprayed again. Not only did I not want to bathe in the perfume of death, but it was also late at night, and I didn't want to deal with it. This would take some creative problem solving for an area in which I have no expertise.

It took several attempts to get him out of the chicken coop. Some were hilarious, ill planned, and did not achieve the intended goal. A water bottle full of hot water squirted repeatedly at his head eventually delivered an eviction notice. Slowly and carefully, he made his way out of the chicken area. No spray, no stink. I'm pretty much an expert on skunk removal now.

You may not be a farmer but you can probably relate to the idea of doing things you don't like. Even though it is our calling, student ministry often pushes us to do things that we haven't been educated for or trained to do. While many moments in ministry are glorious, there are a few that feel a bit lackluster.

For example, we may be asked to complete tasks we feel overqualified to do. A friend of mine tells a story about a new minister at his church who felt he was too educated for a few odd jobs. In one situation, the newbie actually said the words, "I don't load the coke machine. I have a master's degree." If you ever feel that you are too educated or experienced to do a particular task, put down this book, and take a long hard look at your heart. Remember, we serve a Lord who used His final hours to put on a towel and wash His disciples' feet.

Most of us don't think we are overqualified for menial tasks. But we often handle things we don't like to do in one of two ways—we either ignore it and hope it doesn't hurt later, or we hustle through it just to get it done, unconcerned with quality. Some tasks aren't enjoyable because they can be difficult. Decision making, vision, follow up, and difficult conversations can be intimidating. Doing the things that we don't like gives us the opportunity to be better, stronger, and more mature. If we are not ardent about the call God has given us, we will relent when difficult things come our way.

This is not an attempt to paint everyone in the same brush stroke. Different skills and passions determine what we like and what is comfortable for us. With that in mind, there are aspects of student ministry that aren't loved by everyone. This isn't an exhaustive list, but some of these may strike a chord with you.

HANDLING MONEY

For many, numbers aren't that fun, unless of course, we are counting how many students showed up or how many gave their lives to Christ. In that case, numbers are a favorite! Many student ministry friends prefer relationships and investing in others far more than expense reports and tracking receipts.

Budgets and counting dollars are important for a few reasons:

1. **We must plan ahead for financial needs.** How can you decide the price of a trip if you don't count the cost?
2. **You can track where the ministry is spending money and why it is spent.** You may find you spend considerably more in an area than you thought.
3. **You will know how much money you have and how much you are allowed to spend.** Overspending is a bad practice in our personal lives and a horrific practice in ministry.

Get organized and track your receipts. There are quite a few great apps that make it easier. You can even take a picture on your phone, and upload it into a folder in your cloud service to be sure you don't lose it. Tracking receipts isn't fun, but since you are responsible enough to spend the money, be wise in how you account for it.

You have been entrusted with God's money and are a steward of the resources given by those in your church. Many have given sacrificially, trusting that the Lord will use their gifts to further the Kingdom and that is how the budget can exist. Also, that is how your salary is paid. (If you have a salary!) The right view of money will push us to focus on the responsibility instead of the inconvenience in the moment.

> ▶ **PRO TIP**
>
> *Don't wait to be asked for your expense report. You are a professional, so handle your business. Give explanations and be ready to account for what you have spent. If you aren't sure if you should spend the church's money on a particular thing, don't do it. Seek counsel. A clear conscience will save much heartache later.*

You will gain or lose credibility by how you handle money. Managing the budget well is an easy way to gain others' trust and shows you can be trusted with other things. Here's a clear rule: if you won't go over budget in your own finances, you should not overspend with the church's money. How you spend money is a clear indication of how you view stewardship of what God has given you.

Here's one random thought on money and budgets: don't let the fact that you don't have a big budget stop you from doing what God has put in your heart to do. It's easy to complain that you don't have enough. It's way easier to point fingers at the church down the block and say, "If only I had what they have... "

Necessity is the author of creativity and invention. I can speak to this from my own experience. My first year in Miami, we remodeled the student rooms. The budget was low, but expectations were high, as they should be. We had to spend so much money on the important stuff like rewiring electricity, moving air conditioning units, and sound insulation, that it left us with practically nothing for new furniture. It was a big time let down at first.

Our team started brainstorming, it didn't take long to decide what we didn't want. Used couches from Craigslist were out of the question. How could we get furniture for close to nothing? We wrote letters to major companies like Hurley, Billabong, Quiksilver, Volcom, and others. They were beach companies that had a presence in Miami. We didn't beg because we were a church but stated our mission to love and reach students in the community. Any furnishings would be used to help make that happen.

Some companies sent a letter that said they couldn't help. Another sent hundreds of stickers to give students—it was a nice gesture, but you can't sit on stickers. But Heather at Quiksilver called and changed everything. She said they had a warehouse an hour from us that was full of furniture for which they had no plan. *What?* Tell me God can't provide! They gave us tables, coffee tables, chairs, and other stuff we needed. We used much of that stuff for years.

Don't let the budget you have keep you from the dreams God has given you. God knows the size of your budget, and He isn't intimated. Trust Him, work hard, and see where He leads you.

CONFRONTATION

I sat across the restaurant table from a mom who was angry with me. Her daughter had been doing terrible things in student ministry and was confronted. Mom didn't think that behavior was possible and wanted to talk. Mom got irate quickly, surprising me. I had only been in ministry for two years and was learning to navigate these conversations. I didn't really have a plan other than to be nice and tell her the truth. So I did.

It didn't end like I had hoped. She wasn't as angry in the end, but there was no solution to the conversation. That's my fault. I had the responsibility to lead the conversation toward an expected end, if at all possible, and I failed miserably. Fortunately, student ministry provides many opportunities to explain what you are doing and why. With a clear direction for the conversation, tough talks are more navigable.

Restoration must be the goal of tough conversations. Whether you are being confronted or confronting someone else, having a restorative mindset changes everything. Confronting with restoration in mind changes how we speak and view the other person and it gives us a framework for conversation.

The goal of confronting someone is not to win an argument. You can be right and still lose the conversation. Feeling victorious about confrontation doesn't even compare with winning the heart of the other person. A restorative mindset is a graceful reminder of our own failures and shortcomings but highlights the grace God has shown us. We grasp this idea from God through Jesus Christ: We have offended a holy God, yet He wants us to be restored to Him. Look at how Hosea points us to the redemptive, restorative work of the Father:

Come, let's return to the LORD. For he has torn us, and he will heal us; he has wounded us, and he will bind up our wounds.

HOSEA 6:1

These verses tell us the truth of who we are, destroying our self-righteousness, and yet embracing us back. God doesn't hold sin against us or harbor unforgiveness. Restoration-minded confrontation doesn't gloss over sin and wrong doing and it doesn't mean there are no consequences. Rather, it highlights the soul of the person as greater than the offense.

We want those we have to confront to be restored to God and be restored to us. You are a leader and a shepherd. When you confront restoratively, you win a brother or sister. And you teach them what confrontation should be like and how to act accordingly.

TEACHING TOUGH TOPICS

It's easy to shy away from difficult topics when teaching. There are many reasons for this. Ultimately, we don't often teach tough topics because we don't believe the struggle that comes with teaching them will be worth the outcomes.

Our own sin is a barrier to walking through difficult truths with students. If you struggle with pornography, it's easier not to talk about it than to address it in your own life first. If you have racist thoughts, speech, and tendencies, then it will be difficult to share on the all inclusive love God has for all people. The apostle Paul references his approach to teaching the gospel in Acts 20.

Therefore I declare to you this day that I am innocent of the blood of all of you, because I did not avoid declaring to you the whole plan of God.

ACTS 20:26-27

Did you see it? Paul said he was innocent; he had a clear conscience that he had been faithful, not fearful. There was no gray area or holding back, he could put his head on his pillow at night and rest in what had been done.

Teach the whole counsel of the Bible, even when it's tough. You don't have to be like an angry "street preacher"—simply share the truth in love. As the Lord has moved in you, share what God's Word says.

Teaching difficult topics requires dependence on the Word and an absence of opinion. As student ministry leaders, we can become ego centric and somehow gloriously blend the Word of God with our opinion and teach as if they are the same. The truth is, no one is showing up for opinions. The platform is to teach the Scripture, not be on a soapbox. Opinions don't change hearts, only the Word of God can do that.

PRO TIP

Involve parents early if teaching on a controversial subject. This way if mom and dad don't want their student to engage with the topic, they can redirect their student. More importantly, advance warning prepares parents to have conversations when their student gets home. It builds credibility with parents if they know you can be trusted and don't blindside them with difficult topics.

FIRING PEOPLE

Firing someone seems antithetical to working in a church. Can you fire someone from the call God has put on their life? It's important to understand that releasing someone from their role in the church doesn't cancel their calling. However, if the person has had a moral failure, they've disqualified themselves, and this is a consequence.

I hate talking about firing people. Most of us do, and that's why it's often done so poorly. We usually fumble through the process and people are hurt unnecessarily. The conversation about releasing people from employment is far more nuanced than we can cover in this book, but hopefully this discussion will bring about conversation and give you a place to begin. People are let go from a church for many reasons—sin, extreme disrespect, laziness, poor attitude, organizational change, and terrible leadership are just a few.

The first time I had to release someone, I actually had to fire two people at the same time. Many years ago, one of my interns was having an inappropriate relationship with my assistant, both of whom were unmarried. It was heart breaking for them and for me. I loved them both but this wasn't godly behavior. Another intern asked, "Why isn't there grace for them in this situation?" It was a valid question that caused me to reflect. Grace was extended in that we didn't treat them differently or gossip; we sought restoration. The bigger picture is that they were not in a place spiritually to minister to others, they needed to be ministered to. I don't believe they were disqualified from ministry forever, but the focus needed to be on their healing rather than what they could do for the church. If showing grace was to let them keep their jobs, we would have not served them well.

Firing someone is never easy, never enjoyable, and very stressful. I have made mistakes in how I released one or two people, but am convinced I've never fired the wrong person. Here are a few ways to handle the situation properly:

» **Keep a paper trail of offenses for the particular employee.** Document the tough conversations you have had, and make sure the employee understands the severity of what's happening. Make it clear that if the behavior continues, the consequence will be departure from the ministry. This point is important. I once had to release someone that I cared about, and everything about that situation was difficult. Because of my conversations with this person and my background, I thought it was very clear that a pink slip was the next step if the behavior continued. When it was all over, they claimed they had no idea it was coming. I couldn't believe it. It was clear as day to me and others, but not this person. But I didn't have a paper trail, and that was unfair to them.

» **It's bad enough to let someone go, so don't compound the decision with regret.** Ideally, the person being released should never be surprised. They should almost expect it based on conversations and actions that followed up. I've vowed never to make that mistake again.

» **How to handle volunteers.** During some seasons in ministry, some volunteers love to be labeled as part of the team but struggle to follow guidelines or even show up when asked to do so. Sometimes, volunteers may have a bad attitude or be unwilling to pivot in the ministry when needed. So what do you do? Sure, you could "fire" them, but it won't get you the results you're looking for. Rather, consider asking them to take some time off. Lovingly share the offenses with them. Hopefully, this isn't your first discussion about what's gone wrong. If there is a moral failure, then it is most appropriate to ask them to step down from serving. And depending on the severity of the offense, decide if they will be able to serve again. Many volunteers really want to serve but

PRO TIP

Allowing them to make the decision to take some time off keeps you from getting the reputation that you fire volunteers.

either get distracted or can't keep the commitment. By offering them some time off, you give them permission to readjust or step out of the role completely.

CALENDARS

Early is the new "on time." Being consistently late communicates the wrong message to those around you. When you show up late, you are essentially saying that your time is more important than those who are waiting. Does it happen sometimes? Sure it doe. But if a pattern develops, it showcases your disorganization and isn't an isolated incident.

Keeping an up to date calendar doesn't just aid in punctuality, but allows you to make the most of your time and keep your commitments. I've heard it said this way, "You either run your day or your day runs you." That statement continues to be true in my life. Learning to trust your calendar and use it well is a valuable tool. Poor planning leads to wasted time and disappointment. Here are a few tips to help you:

1. **Find a calendar app for your phone that works for you.** It should sync seamlessly with your email, send reminders, and have a user interface that is easy to navigate. If it's too complicated, you won't use it like you should.

2. **Put everything work related on your calendar.** School visits, meetings, lunches, sermon prep, study time, camps, and conferences—everything. If you add them as soon as you are able, it will give a clear picture of your commitments. You cannot balance the tension of work and family if you don't have a plan for how you will work.

PRO TIP

Get an app that will allow you to split professional and personal responsibilities so you can use it in your personal life.

3. **Review your calendar at different intervals.** Plan a few minutes on Sunday night to review the upcoming week. This gives you the opportunity to discuss obligations with your spouse, prepare in advance, and see the gaps in scheduling. If you have a punch list to do or a lunch to schedule, see where you have time in the week and plug them in.

 PRO TIP

Calendar your own personal development time. If you are not in the habit of reading, learning, and studying, this will make sure it gets done. If a task isn't written out, it's less likely to be completed.

Review your calendar before the next work day to prepare for meetings, think through conversations and pray for opportunities. Utilizing a calendar and developing these practices can help you stay organized, complete tasks and goals, inspire confidence from parents, volunteers, and fellow staff, as well as reduce regret.

PREPARING MESSAGES IN ADVANCE

Nightmares are different for everyone. Maybe it's falling from a high place, being chased through the streets, or not getting the last slice of pizza. I've had those, but the most recurring sleep terror I have is that I am asked to speak in church and am not prepared. There I am, standing in front of the people, holding a Bible, and trying to figure it out. It's legitimately horrifying.

What is even more terrifying is knowing there is a responsibility to speak but not preparing for it. This happens way too often in student ministry. You have probably witnessed this as well. It's Tuesday afternoon, and you see a message that says, "Hey, what are you talking on tomorrow night for youth group? Trying to get some ideas." Old school pastors would call that a "Saturday night special." Like cramming for a test last minute, the message is prepared hurriedly and under duress, without contemplation or thought ahead of time.

Bluntly speaking, this is terrible ministry practice. You aren't feeding your students spiritually if you are tossing up hastily prepared messages every week. Once in a while, it happens—you have an emergency or are asked to speak last minute. Other than those moments, it's irresponsible to stand and teach God's Word without preparing and praying about it. Consider this: How would you expect your messages to move students spiritually if it hasn't first moved you? If it hasn't grabbed your attention or wrecked you on some level, how do you communicate with passion and conviction?

We often rely on our giftedness. Lack of preparedness isn't because we don't have time; it's because we think our skill will make up the difference. A college professor of mine said it this way, "A message prepared in the head will reach the head. A message prepared in the heart will reach the heart." The Holy Spirit is the one who moves in hearts and changes lives. That pressure isn't on you or me. The pressure on us is to be communicating clearly and "correctly teaching the word of truth" (2 Tim. 2:15).

CREATE A TEACHING CALENDAR

Sometimes poor planning on a large scale contributes to the issue. Preparation hasn't happened because there is no over-arching plan of what needs to be taught. There is no plan in place, so the tyranny of the urgent drives the topic. Consider creating a teaching calendar for the duration of at least three months to one year. Obviously, the further out you plan, the better. Teaching calendars make room for preparation and creativity. Consistent creativity is difficult in last minute planning.

Gather some of the student ministry team leaders, volunteers, and students. Pray and ask God what students need to learn in the next year. When you are ready, spend four to six hours listing out all the topics, combining ones that are similar, and assigning each topic to a three- or four-week series. Create the sermon focus for each week of the series (including the Scripture is very helpful), and assign creative titles.

The teaching calendar will remove much of the guess work that happens when preparing week to week. Planning in advance does not squelch the voice of the Holy Spirit. Fortunately, He is at work when you're planning ahead. Strategically mapping out teaching actually makes room for the Spirit because there is more time for you to pause and listen. Preparing last minute leaves little room for discernment and plenty of space for chaos. Seek the Lord, gather some people you trust, and prepare so the students can receive the best.

This is the one time a week many students will hear from God's Word. It's during those few moments that

PRO TIP

This is a great time to add creative elements and events that coincide with what's being taught. Assign speakers for each week if you use various people. Align series around holidays, school events, and the rhythm of life. For example, planning a relationship series around Valentine's Day or a "How to share your faith" series right before school starts.

students hear of God's incredible love, forgiveness, and desire to grow in relationship with them. It's an incredibly huge responsibility. We must prepare well and teach to the best of our ability.

Time is of the essence, so consider creating enough margin in your schedule to gather two or three others who love the Word to prepare an outline for the weekly message together. There is great wisdom in a feedback loop. The feedback loop helps answer questions we wouldn't ask on our own. Questions like: Does that illustration work there? Have I shared this story too many times? What are some resources on this subject? What should we call this? Creating lessons in community does not negate the responsibility or role of the leader. Instead, it helps teach and equip others to do the same one day. Don't be threatened to share time creating messages.

Don't just prepare better sermons, present them more effectively. Hone your speaking skills. Have someone video your teaching, and take time to review it. Look for word repetition, intonations, and clarity. Does your body match what your mouth is saying? Are you believable and passionate?

We've been given one opportunity per week and God is sending us students who are desperate to know Him. We must do our very best to present all parts of the gospel clearly and creatively.

MEETINGS

A great meeting doesn't happen by accident. You know this already, though, because you have sat through many meetings that could have been an email or wasted your time entirely. Whether you lead or attend a meeting, get the absolute most out of the time.

If you are attending a meeting, regardless of who is leading it, show up early and ready to contribute and share ideas. Don't walk in, half asleep, with a "Let's just get this over with" mindset. Make the most of your time and engage with what's happening, even when it's difficult. When meeting with your pastor, deacons, or elders, be overly prepared. Know your numbers, and share stories of how God is moving. Be ready to communicate the good that is happening and something that is challenging right now. This lets the room know you are being truthful and not sharing a false narrative.

If you aren't leading the meeting, know your place. Don't be the dominant speaker or try to have all the answers. An intern who once served in our ministry didn't have the ability to "read the room." She had been at our church for five weeks and talked incessantly about how she would do things and how the church would be better if her changes were implemented. She had to be coached on how, when, and what to talk about.

> **PRO TIP**

Don't speak flippantly on areas in which you aren't well informed.

Gathering people to meet is a costly affair; it's not just time, it's money. Remember there are no one hour meetings. It's one hour times the number of people in the room. If your meeting has four people, it's a four hour meeting. If those people are on payroll, it becomes expensive pretty quickly. Consider time and money when you ask people to meet with you. Don't have meetings just to have a meeting. Create the type of meeting that benefits your team. If your meeting is helpful and insightful, it will be worth attending and engaging. Keep these parameters in mind to add value to your meetings:

> » **Send the agenda ahead of the meeting.** Two things happen when you do this: you have prepared for the meeting and you have prepared the attendees. Giving out the topic of conversation ahead of time allows your people to process what will be discussed. They can brainstorm, prepare necessary data, and be ready to contribute. If they're surprised by what's being discussed, the meeting will take much longer than necessary.

> » **Have a compelling reason for the meeting.** If you aren't convinced that an in-person gathering is the best way to handle what's necessary, then send an email. By the way, you can only do a few "It's good to get everyone together" meetings before they get stale. The reason for the meeting drives the content and the conversation.

> » **Have a time of teaching or encouragement.** Use a few minutes of your meeting to share what God is teaching you and how it impacts ministry. Most people want to hear how God is working in their leader's life and the transparency helps them to look for God in ministry life. Also, take a few minutes to share what you're learning about ministry or leadership. An excerpt from a book you've read, podcast, or a conversation that will help sharpen your team is always good. This part of the meeting helps your team feel like they benefit from the meeting; it's not just something else for them to do.

> » **Take time to celebrate.** This is hugely important. Celebration is encouraging and reminds people of the vision. When the pre-meeting agenda is sent out, ask the participants to come ready to celebrate something. Whether it's ministry related or personal, celebration lightens the mood and gives us a chance to cheer each other on.

» **Leave with action steps.** Collaboration, brainstorming, and planning are all great meeting attributes, but if ideas are only discussed and there is no plan to execute, then the meeting was a complete waste of time. Before the meeting ends, assign clear next steps from what was discussed. Name the person who should complete each task, their next step in the process, and the timeline to accomplish it. This way, when the team leaves the meeting, they know what's expected of them and how their goals will be accomplished.

DUE DILIGENCE IN PROTECTING STUDENTS

Careful attention must be given to the details of recruiting the right volunteers who love Jesus and love students. We must be able to look parents in the eye and say with confidence that we are doing everything possible to protect and provide for their student. This process can be tedious and time consuming, so most ministry leaders aren't rushing to another seminar on how to keep their ministry safe. But maybe they should be.

» **Background checks are an absolute must have.** Further, they should be national checks, not just regional or local background checks. Moving across the country is very commonplace, and it's important to evaluate each person as closely as possible. You would definitely want to know if a soon-to-be leader has charges against them in another state.

» **Applications to serve are also important.** These ask personal questions and give history about the person's life. Questions about past indiscretions or habits can be answered by the applicant. References are very helpful in the onboarding process as well. Consider calling three people who can vouch for the potential leader in the areas of integrity and lifestyle. If hiring staff, talking to someone at their previous church is an absolute must.

None of this is fun, which is why it's often neglected. From experience, when you are in a courtroom on the witness stand in front of a judge, you will be glad you didn't skip due diligence. How frightful it would be to look at a situation like that and know it could have been avoided if only you had followed through.

Some aspects of ministry are considerably more enjoyable than others. Don't neglect the parts you don't like or feel comfortable with. When we engage with and excel in areas that we don't like, we will grow as individuals and our ministries will benefit.

» QUESTIONS

1. Name a couple of things in student ministry that you do not enjoy doing. (Be honest, no one is looking.)

2. How can your leadership improve as a result of doing things you don't like to do?

3. How can your ministry benefit as a result of you starting or improving something on the list you made in Question 1?

4. How is your due diligence process? Do you feel you can look a parent in the eye and say, "We are doing everything we can to keep your student safe"?

10 ▸ A NEW SCORECARD

> "The big question about how people behave is whether they've got an Inner Scorecard or an Outer Scorecard. It helps if you can be satisfied with an Inner Scorecard."[1]
>
> **WARREN BUFFET**

MATTHEW EMMONS WAS JUST ONE SHOT AWAY from winning his second Olympic gold medal. Emmons, considered an elite marksman in the 50 meter rifle category, was all but guaranteed first place and the top position on the winner's platform.

He took his position and lowered the barrel of the gun toward the target. Inhale. Exhale. Pause. BOOM! Bullseye! Emmons nailed the middle of the target. What should have been an eruption of celebration was met with disbelief. He received no medal; he wasn't even a close second. Rather, he sank to eighth place in the competition.

After pulling the trigger, Matthew realized his mistake. Though he was aiming directly at the bullseye, he made one major miscalculation: he was aiming at the wrong target. He said, "I didn't look at the numbers above the target before the last shot. ... I should have looked."[2]

What a painfully difficult lesson to learn. The years of practice, discipline, and execution came down to one moment and a simple lack of focus, changing the outcome forever. Emmons' aim was all that mattered and on that day he came up short. This true story is a powerful parallel for us in ministry life: where we set our sights determines our destination.

Our aim, like Emmons', is vital to our success. We have fixed our sights on ministry and want to see students lives changed. Our goal is to help students to surrender to Jesus, change the world, and become disciple makers. Paul employs a different analogy for our spiritual journey, using the idea of a race. In this passage, he eluded to that day we will stand before God and give an account of how we stewarded what we were given in this life.

Don't you know that the runners in a stadium all race, but only one receives the prize? Run in such a way to win the prize. Now everyone who competes exercises self-control in everything. They do it to receive a perishable crown, but we an imperishable crown. So I do not run like one who runs aimlessly or box like one beating the air. Instead, I discipline my body and bring it under strict control, so that after preaching to others, I myself will not be disqualified.
1 CORINTHIANS 9:24-27

In essence, Paul was saying, "Be sure we hit the right target." You can hit the bullseye on any target, so aim for the right one. It is easy to aim for a perishable crown, for things that don't matter in eternity. So, be certain you aim for things that last. As D. L. Moody said, "Our greatest fear should not be of failure, but of succeeding at something that doesn't really matter."[3] It's humbling to consider working an entire lifetime and have our work be insignificant in eternity.

Have you ever considered what you're aiming for? The spiritual answer is, "The glory of God!" I would agree with you, but is that honestly true all of the time? Most of us probably strive to make everything we do for the glory of God and hope it will make an eternal impact—and much of our work does. But it could also be argued that we sometimes battle to stay focused on the true target. There are many distractions that captivate us and seemingly provide faster, more fulfilling results.

THE NUMBERS GAME

I mentioned measuring ministry by numbers in Chapter 6, but didn't delve into the ugly side of numbers. A healthy ministry should be a growing ministry. However, there's a dark side of counting the amount of seats filled. While it's good to keep track of numbers, numerical growth by itself isn't a win. Here are some of the warning signs of "winning" by numerical growth:

» **Your heart is satisfied, and you feel complete and affirmed when you see increased attendance.**
» **Seeing impressive totals on reports gives you a feeling of dominance, and you might even get a sense of satisfaction thinking of other ministries that are not growing like yours.**
» **You may even feel compelled to share data on social media to make sure everyone knows what God is doing in your ministry.**
» **You might greet students when they arrive by asking why they didn't bring a friend but neglect to address them personally.**

If you treat the staff and volunteers around you like a position on an organizational chart designed to complete your task, then your focus isn't being a shepherd: it's on counting sheep. One key indicator that you are placing too much emphasis on who shows up is that you can't wait to ask other ministry leaders about their numbers so you can tell them yours. After all, "It's all God"—but He really doesn't get mentioned that much.

In this scenario, the opposite is also true. If numbers aren't at the pace you expect, then you feel something is wrong with you or the people that you serve along side. You're upset, bothered, and will do whatever is necessary to improve, including mistreating others to get what you want.

If cramming as many students as possible into your space is your end goal, then you probably aren't concerned with their continued spiritual formation. This is the dark side of numerics. Many student ministry leaders aren't nearly as consumed with what happens in students' lives when they are outside of the church walls.

If this sounds familiar, then you're aimed at the wrong target. You're probably amazing at what you do, but you have missed the point. The effects of your work may produce some eternal fruit, but make no mistake, your efforts weren't for the glory of God.

COMPARISON

Comparison is a killer. It's a game with no winners—you will lose every time. When I arrived at my first church, fresh out of college, we had six students in attendance on Wednesday nights. I interned at a large church, so I expected to see it grow. In those days, when group size was mentioned, I would be embarrassed about how many students showed up. I didn't want my ability as a pastor judged by the number of students who walked through the door.

But it wasn't just the numbers. I looked at other student rooms—their bands, lights, and so on—and I would make a negative comment to myself about how they must "need all that stuff." I became bent on showing that I could grow a ministry without all the attractional stuff that our church just couldn't afford. I was jealous of bigger churches and there was no justifiable reason for it.

I always thought "those" guys at the bigger churches had it easy. Unlimited funds, tons of volunteers, and probably way less work each week—or so I thought. I wrongly believed the larger churches were trying to "steal" my kids because I was concerned with depth and they only cared about attendance. I had no idea how wrong I was and how much my heart needed to change. I was motivated by comparison, and that mindset stole an unbelievable amount of joy from me. I have no idea why I had that attitude. I truly believe that I missed some good friendships and opportunities during that time.

If some of this sounds familiar, comparison is killing you. Comparison is pride on display. The bitterness, anger and gossip involved with trying to level up with someone else is ultimately soul crushing. The new target shouldn't be comparing yourself to others, but working together for the sake of the gospel. As my friend Wil says, "Collaboration beats comparison any day."

APPROVAL

It's normal to need affirmation and be encouraged by it—approval can even help us and inspire us to keep working hard. However, the applause of others becomes deadly when it consumes us.

Approval is a moving target. All people have a desire for affirmation, so it can be tempting to think something like this: "Someone noticed me—I am doing well. I need to do more of that." Before long, we are looking for others to affirm our work for God, rather than to God alone. We are hustling to be noticed by others.

Here are a few indicators that you're aiming for the approval target:

» **You share your wins every chance you get—even when no one asks.** It's a compulsion: you believe others need to know that you are winning. The bigger the numbers or more impressive the information, the better. Even if some numbers are "fudged" a bit, it's OK. People will be encouraged by what "God" is doing through you.

» **You speak grandiose and "not quite true" statements to impress others.** I knew a youth pastor who was a great speaker. He spoke at a camp or two in the summer, either in his home state or one nearby. However, on stage when speaking, he would say things like, "I speak all over the country." It just wasn't true—not even close. It seems harmless, but the phrasing deceptively painted a much bigger picture than reality. Another version of this is playing acquaintances as friendships or using the names of "famous" people so it seems like you run in the same circles.

» **You won't ask for help.** Believe it or not, there is yet a darker side to all of this. Approval dictates that we perform well all the time, so having issues is out of the question. There is no room for transparency and needing help. This perspective paints needing help as a weakness and an inability to do what's been asked. What's the unfortunate response to this thought process? Put your head down, work harder, and get over it.

This dangerous numbers game, along with comparison and our need for approval are rooted in our pride. Let's just be real: pride is sin. Usually, we gloss over these issues in ministry as long as the desired outcomes are met. It's not until something blows up in our faces that we seek help.

As leaders with integrity, we can't overlook these behaviors. While we may not consider these as bad as some more obvious sins, these "hidden" sins are just as deadly. These things are not indicators of an healthy shepherd. Is it feasible for a spiritually and emotionally unhealthy leader to lead emotionally healthy people? Could these behaviors be the outward expression of an internal brokenness that has yet to be redeemed?

The emotional, psychological, and spiritual toll of aiming at the wrong target is beginning to show fruit. Look around: there are pastoral casualties every where. We are in ministry to bring God glory with our lives. We all look forward to the day when we hear the words, "'Well done, good and faithful servant! You were faithful over a few things; I will put you in charge of many things. Share your master's joy'" (Matt. 25:21).

If all of the numbers on paper are good and you receive applause from others, it doesn't necessarily mean you hit the right target. If you have been miserable, insecure, mistreated people, hurt your friends and family, or put yourself on a pedestal, is that well done? Is that what God is talking about? Is that the life that He called us to?

THE ETERNAL SCORECARD

Jesus has some different ideas for us concerning what it means to serve Him.

> *"Come to me, all of you who are weary and burdened, and*
> *I will give you rest. Take up my yoke and learn from me,*
> *because I am lowly and humble in heart, and you will find rest*
> *for your souls. For my yoke is easy and my burden is light."*
> **MATTHEW 11:28-30**

One day we will all stand before God, and our own good works and righteousness will have no value. Our best laid plans, attendance reports, church comparisons, and all of our accolades will be in the past. I'm not completely sure what those moments will be like when we stand in front of Jesus, but it's hard to envision God saying, "Well done," if our scorecard has focused completely on us. If we are going to have the right scorecard at the end of this life, it's imperative that we identify what we're doing to inflate our egos and what matters in eternity.

Do numbers matter? Absolutely, each one represents a soul that is precious to God. Is it wrong to want to win and be excellent? Of course not. You should want to win in whatever you do and strive for excellence. Is it a problem that I need affirmation? No, we all need it. We just can't allow the approval of others to be our motivation.

I'm sure you're asking, "Why all of this negative commentary?" To be honest, I don't enjoy it either, but that doesn't mean it isn't necessary. If we can be truthful about our motivations and what we consider a "win," then we can focus on what really matters.

A NEW TYPE OF SCORECARD

My sons played one season of basketball in a recreational league. This league gave kids an opportunity to learn and play the sport, but our time in it was short-lived because of my love for scorecards. You see, this league did not keep score. The emphasis was on playing and learning, not winning.

I'd like to say that I love that approach, but I don't. I kept the score for my kid's games and would tell them the score when appropriate. I just couldn't fathom running, practicing, doing drills, and playing games without having any idea if you were getting better or not. After that season, we enrolled them in the more competitive city leagues. A scoreboard isn't everything, but it shows progress or the lack thereof.

HOW SCORECARDS HELP

The idea of a scorecard doesn't sit well with all ministry leaders. For some, it seems too corporate, and they feel that it inhibits the work of the Holy Spirit. Others just don't like accountability, and the idea of "keeping track" just feels like more work. But there are those who love having a scorecard because it keeps them pointed in the right direction. There's no confusion about where time should be spent because that's determined by the scorecard. They just have to execute the plan.

A scorecard helps us make sure that we are wise stewards of the time, resources, and people that God has entrusted to us. Don't be afraid of having a scorecard; be afraid of winning at the wrong things. Perspective is important.

THE CHALLENGE: CREATING A NEW SCORECARD

I want to challenge you to consider a new scorecard for your ministry because every moment matters. A scorecard gives us a healthy respect for the day when we will look back over our lives. I don't want to stand in regret for not loving others well and wasting time on things that don't matter. I really do want to hear, "'Well done, good and faithful servant'" (Matt. 25:21). A scorecard helps keep our attention in the right places. This new student ministry scorecard should celebrate all aspects of spiritual growth, not necessarily just the easily identifiable.

Lag and lead measures also help us to understand the scorecard better. Lag measures track the success of your scorecard. Let's use the example of attendance at student services. Obviously, we want our ministry to grow, so that is a goal. The actual number of students that show up is the lag measure, or the result.

Lead measures show the activity or strategy it takes to actually complete the lag measure. Continuing the example of attendance, the lead measures would be how you will attract and engage students to attend your services. Lead measures help us get to the desired lag measure (scorecard) we are praying for. Let's look at some lag measures for a new student ministry scorecard, then consider some lead measures on how to complete them.

Salvations

Salvation decisions are a great goal on the scorecard. It's not just the number of decisions that matters, but that students are surrendering their life to Christ in your ministry. It's important for this to be part of the score because it clarifies a few things.

» **It shows that you are clearly presenting the gospel and giving students an opportunity to respond.** If you only talk about salvation but never give students a chance to answer to the movement of God in their hearts and experience conversation, then you are holding them back.

» **Salvations also indicate there are most likely guests coming to your ministry.** When there have been no decisions for a long time, it could be there are no more lost students there to hear the good news you are presenting. Some tough questions must be asked at this point. Do you have an inviting and welcoming culture? Do your students understand how to live and share the gospel?

Baptisms

Baptisms are a tangible sign of the new believer's commitment to Christ. We know there are so many challenges to a student being baptized. Parent's permission, cultural views of baptism, and timing can hinder a student from following through. This is an important part of the score because it shows us that:

» **Students understand and embrace following Jesus.** They understand that a public declaration of their faith sets them apart, and they are willing to accept accountability for how they live.

» **If students are not being baptized, then there must be some evaluation as to why it's not happening.** Has baptism been discussed and taught on so it is understood? Are students being followed up with immediately after their salvation decision? Are parents being included in the conversation so there is clear understanding? Do you celebrate baptisms so there is a culture of praising God when it happens?

Discipleship

Discipleship is the clear next step for all believers. Being baptized isn't the finish line; it's the starting line for a life that honors God and a faith that is growing. Discipleship is intentional investment from a mature Christ follower to help others grow with God. We discussed this in Chapters 6 and 7, but here's why it belongs on the score card.

>> When leaders disciple students, they are following the example of Jesus and making spiritual growth a priority.
>> When students make disciples, it shows it's actually in your culture and not just something said from stage.
>> When discipleship is happening, even when its not on the church calendar, the scorecard shows that your ministry talks about it, teaches it, and gives students opportunities to grow.

If discipleship is not happening, we must ask ourselves a few key questions.

>> How is discipleship talked about from stage?
>> Are there tangible ways for students and leaders to be discipled?
>> Is there a strategy for discipleship?
>> Has the leader of the ministry ever been discipled?

Leaders Carrying Out Vision

Leaders carrying out the vision is a great indicator of ministry health. This showcases that those who are volunteering believe in what's being taught and engage students accordingly. When leaders aren't clear about the vision, volunteers often suggest new directions or constantly question leadership. Keep track of how leaders are engaging because it is a direct reflection of your leadership.

When leaders live out the vision, ministry gets done and students lives are impacted. Volunteers trust their leader and believe that what they are doing is valuable and worthy of their time. If leaders aren't carrying out the vision, consider a few things.

>> Have you been absolutely clear with the vision for the ministry?
>> How often do you train volunteers?
>> Do you keep in regular contact with them so they feel like they are part of a team?

Students Sharing the Gospel

Students sharing the gospel without it being on the calendar shows the effects of disciple-making. We celebrate when students grasp the depths of the forgiveness they have experienced and commit to sharing that with someone else. Obedience to Jesus' commands reveals the growth the student is experiencing.

Personal Life

Loving your family well and doing well in ministry is the personal part of the scorecard and it's important. Honestly, you can nail every part of your scorecard and fail at this one. The ministry "sweet spot" is to do well in ministry and know you are loving your family well also.

Family should always come before ministry, but don't ever hide behind your family instead of doing work. There will always be times and seasons of tension in ministry, but those can be navigated with communication and planning.

Regret happens when you choose to love ministry more than your family. Your spouse and children may resent that you are in ministry because you are always gone or even absent when you are present. Consider where your time is spent and why. Ask your family to give their honest opinion of your work schedule. Evaluate your time and make the most of your work days.

It's a new day in student ministry and a new scorecard is required. We want to see students come to Christ, live as disciple-makers, and raise up a family who loves Jesus. Aim for the right target. Love Jesus, deny yourself, work intently, and love well. Let's stand together before the throne one day and hear the words, "'Well done, good and faithful servant'" (Matt. 25:21).

» QUESTIONS

1. Define your current scorecard. What's most important right now?

2. What is your dream scorecard? What do you value as important?

3. Numbers are important because they represent people. How and where in your ministry do you currently track numbers? What do you do with that data?

_____
_____
_____
_____
_____
_____
_____
_____

4. Would you add anything to the scorecard list? If so, what? Explain.

_____
_____
_____
_____
_____
_____
_____
_____
_____
_____
_____

11 BEFORE YOU GO

"If you don't like something, change it. If you can't change it, change your attitude."[1]

MAYA ANGELOU

WHEN GOD CALLED MY FAMILY AND ME to leave Miami and serve at Long Hollow just outside of Nashville, my world seemed upside down. We loved Miami—our church, our friends, the culture, the food, and the ocean felt like they were custom made for us. We had witnessed God move amazingly in our church and south Florida, where 78.8 percent of the over 4 million people are lost.[2] There were people far from God everywhere we went. I planned to grow old in ministry, retire, and hang out on a boat doing more ministry.

We had happily said no to other opportunities in the past, expecting that we would probably say the same thing when my now pastor called. We said we would pray, but weren't convinced we were going anywhere. God had other plans. He gave us peace to start a conversation, visit the church, talk with the leadership team, and ultimately make the move. What seemed distant and impossible became a reality. We believe God had called us to serve in Miami, and we weren't going to leave until we felt like He had released us. There was both a "push" to leave Miami because the time was right and a "pull" to Nashville as a result of the Lord's calling.

Change in ministry is unique from other jobs. As a ministry leader, it's not just a job. You invest deeply in the lives of the people you serve. When leaving a ministry position, it feels like you're severing relational ties that took years to foster.

Most likely, you will experience a role shift in the future. I'm not wishing that for you, but statistics show it's a very real possibility. For some, change may be more of an adjustment, like stepping into another position inside the same church. It will hurt to move away from the people you have invested in directly, but since there is no relocation, community can continue.

More dramatic shifts may include retiring from ministry, which happens so rarely that it would be an honor to finish that way. Other ministry leaders step out of ministry because of life change or because God changes their desires. Don't live in fear that you may experience changes one day. Instead, have a strategy and be prepared for when you feel God is moving that way.

COMMIT TO PRAYER

Before even considering making a move, seek the Lord. If you believe He is the One who brought you to your current location, He will be the One who releases you.

Learning facts about the new location can be an influence early in the decision making. Be careful that location, salary, proximity to family, and serving with friends don't become the defining factors in your move. Those are all incredible possibilities, but they shouldn't guide the decision.

Commit to praying consistently before each phase of the process.

>> Should you consider leaving?
>> Do you have peace about going?
>> Is this the place to consider?
>> Should we go there?
>> How do we leave well?

The prayers of people who love God are powerful (Jas. 5:16). Don't let prayer be the bookend after the decision is made. The confidence that God—not your emotions—led your decision will be irreplaceable on the difficult days which are sure to come.

FOLLOW GOD'S LEADING

Leaving a current ministry position for another is a significant change in life plans. It's not just leaving a job; it's leaving people who you have invested in for years and have become like family. There are a number of reason for leaving a ministry role, see if any of these resonate with you.

1. **Promises weren't kept which leads to disillusionment.** There are horror stories of churches making promises that they have no intention of keeping. Continued education, benefits, and other deals made at the time of hiring weren't honored and will not be. How do you work for someone who won't keep their word?
2. **There is distrust for church leadership.** This may involve shady dealings or questionable behavior, but ultimately leadership is behaving in such a way that casts doubt on their integrity. Can you follow someone you do not trust?
3. **A change in vision or direction that doesn't match up with personal convictions.** Sometimes this involves doctrinal issues, sometimes it's merely the philosophical approach to doing ministry. If you cannot lay your head on your pillow at night with a clear conscience, evaluation is necessary.
4. **Opportunity for personal growth somewhere else.** Resist the urge to discount this reason; it's not as unspiritual as it may sound. The desire to grow and continue learning isn't fleshly. A church or leader may be content to leave you in a role because you are doing a great job, then resist other opportunities for you because they may not be able to easily replace you. Other times the senior leader is a "leadership lid," and no other opportunities will be available. It is difficult to know in your gut that God has more for you but it cannot happen in the current situation.
5. **Leaving the leader.** Marcus Buckingham, author and consultant, said this, "People leave managers, not companies."[3] Most of the time, this is an accurate statement. If leaders don't lead well or mistreat their people, why stay? Growing leaders are frustrated by immaturity.

If you're considering a change in your future, know that it's never easy and should never be taken lightly.

LOYALTY AND COMMITMENT ARE EASY WHEN YOU ARE WINNING

When the ship is sinking or the team is losing, loyalty and commitment are often the first things to go. Difficult times make you dig deep to consider what is worth fighting for and seem to enhance your reasons for departure.

Don't let one tough season of ministry make you leave. There will be tough seasons at the next place too. Nowhere is perfect, regardless of what you are told. I heard a lady from Louisiana say, "The grass is greener on the other side because there is more poop there." As a farm owner, I know the truth of this statement in farming. As someone who's been in ministry for over 20 years, I also know the truth of this statement in ministry. If there isn't moral failure or something drastic, don't throw in the towel too quickly. Learning to navigate difficulty will sharpen you, and the people will be encouraged by your presence. Be a catalyst for change if possible instead of leaving being your first response.

DON'T LEAVE ANGRY

Being hurt in church leadership feels different than other types of relational pain. Ministry leaders aren't supposed to be vindictive and spiteful, but it happens from time to time. Few things hurt as deeply as being wounded by those you have poured your life into and served or served with.

Do your best to resolve anger before leaving. It won't be easy, but it is worth it. Carrying anger to your next assignment will only cause bitterness, hatred and distrust for others. Harboring those feelings will keep you from doing all that God has for you.

Have conversations with the offending parties to seek restoration. It's a bold move, one that most would rather ignore. Lord willing, there will be restoration in the relationships and you can have peace. Worst case scenario, you will have honored God and shared your heart. There still may be some hard feelings, but the healing process for you can begin much sooner.

THERE SHOULD BE A PUSH AND A PULL

A push can be described as peace from God knowing that it's time to leave your current role. It's the right time, being done in the right way, and there are no regrets in how the departure is playing out. A pull is a tug from the future location. You sense that's where God is leading you and the opportunity seems right.

If there is only a "pull" to make a change, it usually indicates unhappiness at the current location. Only having a pull is synonymous with running away from a situation and sets a dangerous precedent for dealing with issues. In this context, it's easy to look at any other opportunity as "the Lord's will" because it gets you out of the one you are in. The presence of a push and a pull places you in an emotional healthy place to follow the Lord's leading.

PRAY FOR GOD TO OPEN AND CLOSE DOORS

Weighing opportunities causes us to lean on the Lord in unique ways. We listen closely for His voice and yearn to follow His lead. It's a sweet time of listening closely to the Lord's leading as you wait on Him. Ask God to make it obvious where He wants you to go. Ask Him to close the doors that are not where He is leading and to open doors where He sees fit. I'm not saying you need a "fleece" like Gideon, but rather petition Him to give you a heart for where He wants you and a distaste for where you should not be.

SEEK COUNSEL

Don't make decisions in isolation, especially one of this magnitude. There is a wealth of wisdom from people who have transitioned before you who can help you discern the right decision. Walking with trusted friends through this process brings wisdom and comfort. It's also biblical. Scripture shows us the importance of including others in our decision making process. Take a look:

Without guidance, a people will fall,
but with many counselors there is deliverance.
PROVERBS 11:14

GOD WILL SPEAK TO BOTH OF YOU

If you are married, God will confirm the new direction to you and your spouse. Resist the temptation to ignore what your spouse is saying. God often uses them as a voice of wisdom as we charge headlong into opportunity. When we move at ministry pace, it's easy to leave others behind as we make decisions quickly. This is not one of those times. If in fact God is calling you to leave and go elsewhere, He will make it clear to your spouse also.

LEAVE WELL

When you know for sure that God is moving you somewhere else, be sure to finish strong at the place you are now.

GIVE THE CHURCH AS MUCH NOTICE AS POSSIBLE

I've left two ministry positions and neither was easy. At my first ministry role, I let the pastor know that I would be transitioning out in two months. I thought we would let the church know a couple of weeks ahead of time, but he thought differently. On a Sunday morning, I stood on a stage and told the church I would be moving in seven weeks. Man, that was tough. Hanging around that long made it awkward, but I knew I did the right thing by letting the pastor know.

As soon as you know you are moving on, let the pastor know. Get counsel and use wisdom on the exact time, but give enough advance warning for them to accept and adjust. Give them at least two weeks notice that you are leaving.

I've heard stories of pastors leaving in the middle of the night. Don't do that—show love and respect to the people who have loved you (and even those who didn't). Leaving that way leaves a door wide open for rumors and innuendo. Don't let things be left open to interpretation if possible.

On the flip side, leaders who are insecure sometimes get angry when you tell them you're leaving. They may ask you to go ahead and leave and not serve out your last two weeks. If this happens, comply with his wishes and rest assured that you still did the right thing.

PRO TIP

Get a feel for how your boss will respond to your departure. If they will support your move, let them know when you are interviewing. If you sense they will be angry, it's best to wait until you have the job to share.

WORK AS HARD ON YOUR LAST DAY AS YOU DID ON YOUR FIRST DAY

One temptation when leaving a ministry role is to check out and put ambition in neutral. There is no sense of urgency, sometimes becoming undependable, and it's clear to everyone else your heart is already somewhere else.

If you are still getting a paycheck, that church is still the place where you are living out your calling. Work as hard as you did before, if not more so. The focus of your work may change some. If nothing else, work on the hand-off to the next person to make it easier for them. Share plans, forms, documents—whatever is necessary for them to succeed. After all, you still care for the students, parents, and volunteers you've poured yourself into, right?

SAY SOMETHING NICE OR DON'T SAY IT AT ALL

You may have legitimate reasons for leaving, maybe even as a result of things that aren't good. However, it's not your place to share leadership issues and disagreements with church people on your way out the door. Obviously, moral failures are different than disagreements. Don't use your platform to rip apart a church as you leave.

Speak life to people as you talk to them. Encourage them by what you have witnessed God doing through your church. Paint hope for them by reminding them of who they are and who they could be. Transitioning well will prepare you for the next phase of ministry and all that God has for you. Allow the times of prayer, trust and difficulty to shape you as you shepherd elsewhere.

RESOURCES

I want to challenge you to continue to grow in your relationship with God and develop yourself as a leader. Our families, our volunteers, and our students benefit greatly when we devote time to growing ourselves.

This list is by no means exhaustive, but here are a few resources that have helped me along the way. As always, we may not agree with everything that is said, but discernment helps us know what is good and right. I can suggest each of these with full transparency because they are not paid advertisements—they've truly been helpful.

THE ENNEAGRAM TEST

This version is $10, but it's one of the best I've ever participated in. You will have a far better understanding of yourself with a test like this one. Go to https://www.wepss.com.

AUDIBLE

Audible is an audio book company with an incredible selection. It's $16 a month, which is cheaper than buying most books. There's a feature that allows you to record 30 second clips, so if you're driving or cutting the grass, you can "take notes" without stopping. If you find it difficult to read a book, listening to them is super helpful.

BOOK SUMMARY

If you want the content of a great book but don't have the time to read the whole thing, a book summary is a great option. (If you are this far into my book, my gratitude is endless!) A good summary will make an entire book around 12-15 pages. There is a fee, usually monthly, for the service; however, it's a low cost compared to the amount of books you would have access to and be able to read. One example of this is blinkist.com.

PODCASTS

Here are a few shows that I learn from almost every time I listen.

- » *Carey Nieuwhof Leadership Podcast*
- » *The Unstuck Church Podcast* with Tony Morgan
- » *The Lifeway Students Podcast*
- » *Making Disciples* with Robby Gallaty
- » *5 Leadership Questions* by Lifeway

MINISTRY ACTION PLAN

Here's the outline for our church's ministry action plan. Any information is for clarification purposes only.

Name: Jeff Borton   **Campus:** Global

Department: Student Ministry   **Calendar Year:** 2020

» PURPOSE OF YOUR MINISTRY AREA

Student ministry exists to help students know God, find community, make disciples, and change the world by intentionally investing in middle school and high school students.

» PROCESS AND PROGRAMS

Midweek Program

Students offers a weekly service on Wednesday evenings. This service is the first step in our discipleship pathway and is designed to help students know God regardless of where they are on their spiritual journey. A weekly service consists of a dynamic worship experience through music and other creative elements, biblical teaching, and round table discussion to enhance learning and build intentional relationships.

Life Groups

The second step on the Pathway is to participate in a life group. We believe spiritual growth in important. For that reason, we challenge every student to do life with other believers in a life group. Our groups spend time in God's Word through sermon-based curriculum, weekly Bible study, monthly hang outs, and quarterly opportunities to serve together. Groups meet in our student building on Sunday and Wednesday and in various locations around the community throughout the week.

Discipleship groups

Discipleship is an important process for every believer that provides intimate friendships, an environment of accountability, and most importantly, it cultivates a life rooted deeply in God's Word.

The third step in the Discipleship Pathway is to participate in a yearly discipleship group, or a "d-group." A d-group is a gender specific, closed group of three to five believers. In most cases, these groups have an adult leader and meet together weekly for the purpose of accelerated spiritual transformation. The d-group will replicate itself at the end of the time to continue making disciples. A person joins the d-group by invitation only, with most d-groups being formed out of relationships in a life group.

Change the World

Changing the world (missions) is the fourth and final step of our discipleship pathway. Students are given multiple opportunities each year to invest and engage with people from different cultures, circumstances, and beliefs. We change the world by carrying the name of Jesus; investing locally, nationally, and globally; and providing missional opportunities for our students to serve the hurting and reach the lost. Each of these opportunities will stretch students' hearts, minds, and knowledge as they selflessly engage the world.

» ORGANIZATIONAL STRUCTURE

Outline the organizational structure of your ministry including coaches and volunteers.

» SWOT ANALYSIS

Evaluate the conditions of your ministry area through a SWOT profile. The SWOT profile should be used in helping you plan goals for the new ministry year.

- » **S**trengths within the ministry
- » **W**eaknesses within the ministry
- » **O**pportunities for the future
- » **T**hreats to the health of the ministry

» GOALS FOR THE YEAR (EXAMPLES OF MEASURABLE GOALS)

- » **Goal One:** grow weekend services at original campus by 20% and help other campuses do the same.
- » **Goal Two:** move 80% of weekend attendance to small groups.
- » **Goal Three:** increase volunteer recruitment, training and retention.
- » **Goal Four:** launch online student groups. Provide support for local churches.
- » **Goal Five:** launch groups in 15 schools outside of FCA teams.
- » **Goal Six:** host six strategic "sacrifice" weekends for students.
- » **Goal Seven:** increase mission trips.

» TARGETED COMPLETION DATE AND SIGNIFICANT OTHERS

State the goals more succinctly and place a date under each goal for completion. Also, list under each goal the people that will be significant in helping you realize the goal.

» COMMUNICATION AND EXECUTION PLAN

Briefly outline how each goal will be communicated and executed.

» SOURCES

CHAPTER 1
1. "The Sin," The Mandalorian (Disney Plus, November 22, 2019).

2. Howard F. Sugden and Warren W. Wiersbe, *Answers to Pastors' FAQs* (Colorado Springs, CO: NexGen, 2005), 11.

3. John Calvin, *Institutes of the Christian Religion*, ed. John T. McNeill, vol. 1 (Louisville, KY: The Westminster Press, 1960), 108.

4. Emily P. Freeman, *Simply Tuesday: Small-Moment Living in a Fast-Moving World* (Grand Rapids, MI: Revell, 2015).

5. Christine Caine, 2014, "If the light that is in you is not greater than the light that is on you," Facebook, October 5, 2014, https://www.facebook.com/theChristineCaine/posts/if-the-light-that-is-within-you-is-not-greater-than-the-light-that-is-on-you-the/10154679738960089/.

CHAPTER 2
1. Connie Lauerman, "King Gives Wake-up Call to Non-Violence," chicagotribune.com, May 22, 2002, https://www.chicagotribune.com/news/ct-xpm-2002-05-22-0205220139-story.html.

2. "Evangelism Is Most Effective Among Kids," Barna Group, October 11, 2004, https://www.barna.com/research/evangelism-is-most-effective-among-kids/."

3. Ben Trueblood, *Within Reach: the Power of Small Changes in Keeping Students Connected* (Nashville, TN: Lifeway Press, 2019), 18.

4. Tim Elmore and Andrew McPeak, *Generation Z Unfiltered: Facing Nine Hidden Challenges of the Most Anxious Population* (Atlanta, GA: Poet Gardener Publishing in association with Growing Leaders, Inc, 2019), 30.

5. Congressional Medal of Honor Society, "Young Hero Award - Meet Virgil Smith," Facebook (Congressional Medal of Honor Society, December 7, 2019), https://www.facebook.com/CMOHSociety/videos/young-hero-award-meet-virgil-smith/503115510288006/.

6. Elmore and McPeak, *Generation Z Unfiltered*, 30.

7. Kim Parker and Ruth Igielnik, "What We Know About Gen Z So Far," Pew Research Center's Social & Demographic Trends Project, May 14, 2020, https://www.pewsocialtrends.org/essay/on-the-cusp-of-adulthood-and-facing-an-uncertain-future-what-we-know-about-gen-z-so-far/.

CHAPTER 3
1. Willis, Dave (@davewillis). 2014. "Time is the 'currency' of relationships. There's no way to invest into a relationship without investing your time." Twitter, March 20, 2014, 11:15 a.m. https://twitter.com/davewillis/status/446666296495992833.

2. John Acuff, 2018, "Leaders who can't be questioned," Facebook, October 15, 2018, https://www.facebook.com/CatalystLeader/posts/leaders-who-cant-be-questioned-end-up-doing-questionable-things-jon-acuff-cataly/10155517856602035/.

CHAPTER 4
1. Scott Barry Kaufman, "Choose Growth," Scientific American Blog Network (Scientific American, April 7, 2020), https://blogs.scientificamerican.com/beautiful-minds/choose-growth/.

2. Peter Scazzero, *Emotionally Healthy Spirituality: It's Impossible to Be Spiritually Mature, While Remaining Emotionally Immature* (Grand Rapids, MI: Zondervan, 2017), 13.

3. Regan Bach, "Creating White Space: The Key to Increased Creativity and Productivity," Noteworthy - The Journal Blog (Medium, February 5, 2019), https://blog.usejournal.com/creating-white-space-the-key-to-increased-creativity-and-productivity-50af0d1c2811.

4. Ibid.

CHAPTER 5
1. John Maxwell, "Communicating Vision," John Maxwell, June 11, 2011, https://www.johnmaxwell.com/blog/communicating-vision/.

2. CatalystConference, "Andy Stanley | Catalyst Atlanta 2006," YouTube (YouTube,

July 9, 2007), https://www.youtube.com/watch?v=xoigF3COwbE.

3. Eric Schmidt, Jonathan Rosenberg, and Alan Eagle, *Trillion-Dollar Coach: the Leadership Playbook from Silicon Valley's Bill Campbell* (New York, NY: HarperCollins Publishers, 2019), 36.

4. Rick Warren, *The Purpose Driven Life: What On Earth Am I Here For?* (Grand Rapids, MI: Zondervan, 2002), 149.

5. John Maxwell, "The Law of the Lid," John Maxwell, July 19, 2013, https://www.johnmaxwell.com/blog/the-law-of-the-lid/.

6. Eric Geiger, "Ten Differences Between Delegating and Dumpster Leadership," Eric Geiger, May 23, 2016, https://ericgeiger.com/2016/05/ten-differences-between-delegating-and-dumpster-leadership/.

CHAPTER 6

1. Jean-Marie Dru, *Thank You for Disrupting: the Disruptive Business Philosophies of the World's Great Entrepreneurs* (Hoboken, NJ: John Wiley & Sons, Inc., 2019), 24.

2. "Application of Philosophy," SeaWorld Parks & Entertainment, accessed January 13, 2021, https://seaworld.org/animals/all-about/training/application-of-philosophy/.

3. Trueblood, *Within Reach*, 12.

4. Trueblood, *Within Reach*, 12.

5. Trueblood, *Within Reach*, 18.

6. Charles E. Hummel, *Tyranny of the Urgent* (Downer's Grove, IL: Intervarsity Press, 1994), 5.

7. Trueblood, *Within Reach*, 18.

8. Ibid.

CHAPTER 7

1. Robert E Coleman, *The Master Plan of Evangelism* (Old Tappan, NJ: Revell, 1964), 37.

2. BASICSeries, "BASIC Follow Jesus. Francis Chan - 'Clean your room,'" YouTube Video, 1:35 , January 16, 2012, https://youtu.be/bgQ2wiTefmQ.

3. Robby Gallaty, *Marcs of a Disciple:*

a Biblical Guide for Gauging Spiritual Growth (Hendersonville, TN: Replicate Resources, 2016).

CHAPTER 8

1. Craig Groeschel, *Daily Power: 365 Days of Fuel for Your Soul* (Grand Rapids, MI: Zondervan, 2017), June 23.

2. Blake Morgan, "50 Stats That Prove The Value Of Customer Experience," Forbes (Forbes Magazine, September 24, 2019), https://www.forbes.com/sites/blakemorgan/2019/09/24/50-stats-that-prove-the-value-of-customer-experience/?sh=70ac0744ef22.

CHAPTER 9

1. *The Empire Strikes Back*, directed by Irvin Kershner (1980; Los Angeles: 20th Century Fox, 1985).

CHAPTER 10

1. Marcel Schwantes, "Warren Buffett Became a Billionaire by Sticking to 1 Simple Rule of Success (Which Many People Don't)," Inc.com (Inc., May 19, 2020), https://www.inc.com/marcel-schwantes/warren-buffett-rule-of-success.html.

2. "Shot at Wrong Target Costs Rifleman Gold," The Independent (Independent Digital News and Media, October 10, 2011), https://www.independent.co.uk/sport/olympics/shot-at-wrong-target-costs-rifleman-gold-587595.html?amp.

3. Jesse Carey, "12 Of DL Moody's Most Profound Quotes About Faith," RELEVANT, December 27, 2017, https://www.relevantmagazine.com/faith/12-dl-moodys-most-profound-quotes-about-faith/.

CHAPTER 11

1. "Maya Angelou: In Her Own Words," BBC News (BBC, May 28, 2014), https://www.bbc.com/news/world-us-canada-27610770.

2. "Send South Florida," Send Network (NAMB, January 6, 2021), https://www.namb.net/send-network/send-city/south-florida/.

3. Marcus Buckingham and Curt Coffman, *First, Break All the Rules: What the World's Greatest Managers Do Differently* (Washington, D.C.: Gallup Press, 2014), 31.

NOTES